Endorsements

The seer anointing is a current invitation from God for the Church in this hour. It is time for us, like Jesus, to see what our Father in Heaven is doing, and do it! Jon Welton has studied this subject and moved in this realm for many years. In *The School of the Seers Expanded Edition*, he shares insight from the Word of God that will help you grab hold of this anointing.

Patricia King
Extreme Prophetic

Jonathan Welton is brilliant. When he teaches, you remember what he has said. God's Spirit is upon him, and the anointing he carries will impact your life.

Harold R. Eberle
Founder, Worldcast Ministries

We are constantly surrounded by the unseen realm of spiritual forces both good and bad. In his work, *The School of the Seers Expanded Edition*, Jonathan Welton reveals valuable insights on how anyone can sharpen his or her own spiritual discernment. By sharing his precious revelations learned through the study of Scripture, church history, and prayer, Jonathan explains to the conventional Christian how to interact with the unseen realm.

Robert Stearns
Founder/Executive Director, Eagles' Wings Ministries

I have passed on a lot of my gifting and grace to younger men and women in the next generation. Jonathan is one of them. He is prototypical of the prophetic Timothys that I have been honored and privileged to speak into in many countries.

Jonathan is clearly an emerging prophetic gift to the Church. His ability to teach *and* demonstrate the revelatory gifts of the Spirit makes him a true double threat!

Dennis Cramer
President, Dennis Cramer Ministries

Jonathan Welton's *The School of the Seers Expanded Edition* will help you discover that the supernatural can become a normal way of life. In this training manual, Jonathan is speaking from experience, not theory, about the many different aspects of seership. Just as blindness and deafness are serious handicaps in the natural, so are spiritual blindness and deafness in the spirit realm. May you begin to see into the unseen realm as you study this manual.

Gary Oates
Author, *Open My Eyes, Lord*
International Conference Speaker

I have known Jonathan Welton for years and I appreciate the man, ministry, and message. Jonathan teaches what he knows and reproduces his anointing in others. This book is an impartation from a man who carries the message and mantle of a seer. You cannot separate between what Jonathan teaches and who he is; this gifting is in his DNA. *The School of the Seers Expanded Edition* will open the realm of the invisible so you can do the impossible. This is the gift that will bring the Body of Christ into the supernatural realm. My prayer is, "Open my eyes, Lord, so that I might see!"

Leif Hetland
Global Mission Awareness

I have been asking the Lord to raise up the next generation of theologians and teachers who will articulate a theology of the Kingdom with signs and wonders to the Body of Christ in the next season. I believe Jonathan Welton is one those new breed of theologians and teachers. He deeply loves the Body of Christ and he carries an anointing for revelation, teaching, and seeing that the Body needs in order to be properly equipped for the days ahead.

Rev. John S. Baylor Jr.
Masters of Divinity, Fuller Theological Seminary

Jonathan opens the eyes of his readers to the exciting life that is available to those who learn to see the spirit realm. He powerfully unveils Scripture to show how many of the leaders in the Bible were able to see into the spirit realm, commune with God and receive divine direction. Few others have taught that this is possible for us today as Jonathan has in *The School of the Seers Expanded Edition*.

Dr. Art Mathias
President, Wellspring Ministries

Jonathan Welton has a passion for God that overflows into his teaching and ministry. His teaching allows you to view the power of the Holy Spirit through the lens of God's Word in new ways. *The School of the Seers Expanded Edition* will challenge and encourage you to change the way you view the world by opening your eyes to the unseen spiritual realm.

Brian Stebick
Regional Director, CSB Ministries
Bachelors of Biblical Studies Baptist Bible College

THE SCHOOL

of the

SEERS

EXPANDED EDITION

with

INTERACTIVE STUDY GUIDE

THE SCHOOL
of the
SEERS

EXPANDED EDITION
with
INTERACTIVE STUDY GUIDE

*A Practical Guide on How to See
in the Unseen Realm*

JONATHAN WELTON

"Promoting Inspired Lives."

This book and all other Destiny Image, Revival Press, MercyPlace, Fresh Bread, Destiny Image Fiction, and Treasure House books are available at Christian bookstores and distributors worldwide.

For a U.S. bookstore nearest you, call 1-800-722-6774.

For more information on foreign distributors, call 717-532-3040.

Reach us on the Internet: www.destinyimage.com.

ISBN 13: 978-0-7684-4214-4

EBook ISBN: 978-0-7684-8732-9

For Worldwide Distribution, Printed in the U.S.A.

5 6 7 8 9 10 11 / 20 19 18 17 16 15 14

Acknowledgments

I would like to start by saying thank you to my wife, Karen, the most important person in my life. You have been the most profound representation of Jesus I have ever known. Your walk of love, humility, forgiveness, gentleness, and faith challenge me daily. You are the biggest sign in my life that there is a God, because I can see Him in your heart daily. I thank the Lord for such a perfect match for my strengths and weaknesses. The trust that you have in my ability to hear from God causes me to walk in a deeper level of the fear of the Lord.

I would like to honor my parents, Jim and Carolyn Welton. I am so thankful for having parents who are the most humble, affectionate, gentle, kind, and compassionate lovers of God that I have ever seen. I love you both so much.

I would also like to thank the following heroes in the Body of Christ; you have been a tremendous example and influence in my life: Randy Clark, Harold Eberle, Patricia King, Dennis Cramer, Cheryl Schang, Watchman Nee, Kris Vallotton, Bill Johnson, Heidi Baker, Gary Oates, Joe McIntyre, Tommy Tenney, John Shoemaker, Bob Sorge, Leif Hetland, and Lance Wallnau.

Table of Contents

INTERACTIVE STUDY GUIDE

Foreword

Jonathan Welton's book, *The School of the Seers Expanded Edition: A Practical Guide on how to see in the Unseen Realm,* is a helpful study for anyone desiring to grow in the prophetic/seer realm. I believe Jonathan is one of the next generation of prophetic ministers. He is well-read, has a great spirit based in love and grace, walks in humility, and has pursued training and advanced degrees in his pursuit of excellence in his gifting and calling.

Jonathan not only writes about the subject, he also models what he teaches by ministering in churches and conferences in the gifts he has written about. I believe Jonathan has learned a lot about character and integrity through healthy role models that began in his home. He comes from a solid family with healthy relationships. He has watched his parents move in prophecy in church and in their ministry. This is such a great foundation to build upon, and it serves him well in his writing, teaching, and prophetic ministry.

Jonathan is one of the young men I have had the privilege of speaking into and have watched him grow rapidly in his pursuit of God and His purposes. I am excited about him and other young prophetic ministers who are arising in this generation. I believe they will go higher, dig deeper in the Word, and experience more at a younger age than many of the past generations. I believe there is a degree of revelatory teaching coming from this generation that will cause us to see truth that we have missed in the past. I have often echoed what my friend Pastor Bill Johnson has so often said: "Our ceiling is the next generation's floor!"

I am excited to welcome to the public Jonathan's book, *The School of the Seers Expanded Edition.* I know that power to work miracles is dependent on revelation from Heaven. The clearer the revelation, the more faith it creates, and the greater the faith, the more powerful the miracle or the healing. Seeing is a biblical concept and principle. Seeing on the part of God's people continued in the history of the Church. Seeing is important for the Church today. What Jonathan has done is write a book that helps us "see" what is in the Bible, and from that truth discover the right of believers to "see" into the unseen realm.

Evangelist Randy Clark
Global Awakening Ministries
Author of *There Is More!*

Preface

Jonathan is a gifted teacher and a humble leader. As his wife and best friend, I respect him tremendously for the unique anointing he carries and the compassionate heart he has to see every believer rise to the fullness of his or her destiny. His influence in my life and the lives of many of our friends has changed us forever. I still encounter people thanking Jonathan for the profound impact his encouraging words and teachings have had on their lives many years ago. I remember the early days when Jonathan first began to experience the "seer" gifting. I will let him tell you the full story in the following pages, but allow me to share with you my perspective.

Jonathan first began to "see in the spirit" when we were both attending a college-age charismatic youth group in upstate New York. At the time, we were close friends and both passionate for Jesus. I remember Jonathan pulling me aside at youth group to tell me about these strange experiences and what he was "seeing." He seemed to be equally freaked out and excited by what was happening to him. Although he did not openly share these experiences with others for a long time, he felt that he could trust me with this information. I remember listening in awe and wonder.

Jonathan explained seeing strangers walking down the street; some had a light or aura around them, and he knew they were filled with the Holy Spirit. He could see a dark cloud surrounding others, and he knew they were depressed or tormented by demons. Even more exciting to me were the angels they usually radiated light or fire. He could describe the color and style of their garments, their facial expressions, and many other details. Certain angels carried staffs or swords, and some, but not all, had wings. Some angels were the size of men; others stood at eight or ten feet tall or taller. Occasionally, he would see angels who were assigned to specific Christians.

In youth group, when we worshipped the Lord with abandonment, countless angels would flood into the room. They would join with us in praising, singing, and dancing. Sometimes, when the worship was cut off, Jonathan saw them crying, knowing that the will of man had overruled what the Holy Spirit wanted to do. He described these experiences in profound detail, as if he saw them as clearly as he saw me.

Had I not known that Jonathan was an emotionally stable, well-respected leader who knew the Bible better than anyone I had ever met, I would have understandably been more skeptical. Instead, I wanted to know everything. I asked him endless questions: "What do you see right now? Do you see anything around me? Are there angels in this room? How do angels *look* to you? Can you see them physically, like you see me, or are they transparent, as if superimposed over the physical realm? Do you see things in your mind's eye?" Many times during worship, I could not bear my excitement any longer, and I would lean over to Jonathan and whisper, "What's happening in the spirit realm right now? Do you see any angels? Where are they?" Most of the time he kept this information to himself, but if I was lucky, I could prod it out of him, and over time he grew more comfortable sharing with others.

Jonathan began a long journey of studying and writing about this gift, delving into the Scriptures and any book he could get his hands on for deeper revelation. The product of his study, seven years later, is the book you are holding in your hands.

Jonathan is a teacher in the true sense of the word. If there is one trait I respect most about teachers, it is not extensive knowledge, charismatic speaking, or even profound revelation. Although all of that is good, I incline my ear to those who continually submit their minds to the Holy Spirit, holding their knowledge not as a trophy but as a clay vessel that the Lord can mold and transform. Paul says, "Be transformed by the renewing of your mind (Rom. 12:2). I have seen this process eloquently modeled in my husband. Like all true teachers, he has never stopped learning.

Jonathan's experiences opened up a whole new world to me. I believed in angels and a spirit realm before, but his encounters made what I read about in the Bible so much more real. Since those early days, I have learned how to grow in my own discernment, experience the spirit realm, and sense angels. Sometimes I can't help but feel like I have an unfair advantage with a seer as a husband! Of course, as you will read, true discernment goes far beyond the ability to see angels. There is a realm of revelation and experience that God has hidden *for* His children, not *from* them. If you are sincere and hungry, you will find it.

My early fascination and curiosity with the spirit realm is shared by many others, both in the Church and outside it. Most of the questions I pestered Jonathan with are the same questions he receives from people when they first hear about his ability to "see in the spirit." God created us to have an appetite for the supernatural. I once heard it said, "We are not physical beings who occasionally have a temporary supernatural experience; we are supernatural beings having a temporary physical experience." The spirit realm is all around us, and it is more real than the physical realm we live in and experience every day. Whether we believe in it or not, our lives are intricately affected by the invisible spirit realm.

Many people have encountered this unseen realm through the New Age, meditation, or other supernatural experiences. These individuals grasp the reality and power of the spirit realm, but the Church does not understand it and often condemns it. Because there is little biblical teaching in the Church today about the spirit realm, many believers have drifted away from the faith, sometimes hurt or confused, because their hunger for the supernatural was quickly rebuked.

Other Christians in the Church have begun to experience supernatural phenomena, such as dreams, visions, open visions, or seeing angels and demons, but they lack solid biblical teaching and become what we have termed *seer orphans*. These individuals are desperately looking for someone to train them, encourage them, and release them. If the Church does not embrace its "seer orphans," then the New Age movement will.

God is restoring the seer anointing and the gift of discernment to the Body of Christ. Jonathan shows how any Christian can safely and biblically experience the spirit realm through Jesus Christ, who is the source of all Truth. Whether you are a "seer orphan" searching for solid teaching or an individual longing to experience the spirit realm for yourself, this book will give you the tools you need to activate and sharpen your own discernment.

Above all, I pray that you would encounter the Lord beyond all your expectations. In fact, before you begin Chapter 1, I dare you to ask the Holy Spirit to reveal himself to you supernaturally before you finish this book. I am convinced that God will always answer this prayer because He promised to draw near to us when we draw near to Him (James 4:8). May this book create a hunger in you to pursue the presence of God, discover the secrets of God, and open new realms of possibilities that you never dreamed existed!

In Christ,
Karen Welton

Introduction

For many years I have heard Christians talking about angels, spiritual warfare, prophecy, and the spirit realm. There have been multitudes of books written on each of these subjects, with many different teachings for each of them. I have asked myself many times, why write another book on this subject? How can I make it unique?

I am a fervent reader of all books about Christian spirituality and the supernatural. What I really enjoy, though, is finding something fresh, profound, and new. As one who is hungry to pursue more of God, and as a seeker of deep truths in the Word, I am attempting to write a book that no one else has written. My desire is to bring you fresh and deep revelation from the Word.

My goal is to create a practical manual for teaching the typical believer how to interact with the unseen realm. In our daily life, we are surrounded by spiritual forces and activities. However a lack of understanding exists inside the Church about how to interact with this reality. This is disturbing, considering that "New Agers" outside the Church tend to be very comfortable with the unseen realm and sometimes understand truths that the typical Christian hasn't been taught.

The foundation for the teaching in this book is the Word of God along with a personal relationship with Jesus Christ. It is important to remember that satan operates his kingdom by counterfeiting the true Kingdom of God. When making a counterfeit, such as money, the goal is to make the forgery look as much like the real as possible. A counterfeit tries to imitate the truth, yet it will never *be* the truth. Although some of the teachings in this book may seem controversial, by measuring them against the Word of God, we should be able to discern the difference between the truth of the Kingdom of God and the lies of the kingdom of darkness.

A counterfeit looks very similar to the real. We can't run away from the real just because there is a counterfeit. Unfortunately, that is what many Christians have done. You would not throw out your money just because there are counterfeiters in the world. Neither should we throw out understanding the spirit world and operating as born-again spirit beings just because there are counterfeits in the world.

Many Christians consider themselves inadequately equipped to understand deep things of the Spirit or operate in the supernatural. Perhaps this has been the case, but training now exists to bring the Church into maturity. That is the very purpose of the book in your hands—to equip the Body of Christ with the information needed to mature in walking in the supernatural.

Scripture gives confirmation to the idea of training people in the supernatural. Take, for example, the following story from the Old Testament.

In First Kings 19:19-21, Elijah, the famous prophet of Israel, takes on an apprentice named Elisha. There was a significant increase of spiritual power when Elijah went home to be with the Lord, and Elisha received double the anointing that was on Elijah's life (see 2 Kings 2:12-14). In fact, Elisha has exactly twice as many recorded miracles as Elijah. Elisha then took on a servant of his own named Gehazi (see 2 Kings 4:12a).

It is my personal opinion that had Gehazi pursued a double portion of the anointing on Elisha, the Lord would have granted it to him as well. However, Gehazi's greed disqualified him from becoming Elisha's successor (see 2 Kings 5:20-27). He not only was disqualified, but was cursed with leprosy! At this point in the story, Elisha took on a new servant whose name is never revealed, so I refer to him as the "no-name" servant.

When the servant of the man of God got up and went out early the next morning, an army with horses and chariots had surrounded the city. "Oh, my lord, what shall we do?" the servant asked. "Don't be afraid," the prophet answered. "Those who are with us are more than those who are with them." And Elisha prayed, "O Lord, open his eyes so he may see." Then the Lord opened the servant's eyes, and he looked and saw the hills full of horses and chariots of fire all around Elisha (2 Kings 6:15-17).

(Author's note: This portion of Scripture is rich with examples, so you will see it quoted several times throughout this book.)

The intention of this book is to lay a foundation for the Body of Christ to experience what the "no-name" servant experienced. I pray that the Lord would literally open your spiritual sight so that you may see into the unseen realm.

ACTIVATION

An activation exercise follows each chapter to assist you in applying the knowledge you've gained into practice, to help stretch your spiritual muscles, and prepare you to walk in the anointing of seeing in the spirit and discerning of spirits. The truths in this book are deep and stretching. In order to get the most out of this book, I strongly recommend that at the end of each chapter you stop, put in your bookmark, and do the activation exercise. You will receive the best assimilation of this material if you take my advice on this. Most of all enjoy, and have fun growing!

—Part One—
PILLARS

CHAPTER 1

The Mantle of Fire and Water

WHERE IT ALL BEGAN

How would you feel if a well-known prophet stood you up in a church service and prophesied that you would begin to see things in the spirit, that you would have a gift for discerning spirits, and that God would even teach you about being a "seer?" As many of you probably would be, I was excited, confused, and soon-to-be quite freaked out. To give some clarification, I have included the exact prophecy I received from Prophet Dennis Cramer:

March 7, 2002

You're a young man with a tremendous call upon his life, very, very strong call...you have had some rumblings lately of prophetic ministry. And you thought maybe you were losing your mind. You thought, *Lord, my mind is going off. What's wrong with my mind?* You're also a man that is going to begin to discern spirits more than you ever wanted to. So, the Lord told me to tell you, Jonathan, you are not losing your mind; you are simply beginning to discern spirits as never before. There is a good prophetic call upon your life...But also, as I said, especially discerning of spirits.

March 9, 2002

Jonathan, you have a strong seeing edge already developing in your life. You are uncomfortable with this because you don't know what you are seeing. It's caused you some distress. You've almost begun to feel a little rejected. But the Lord says all He is doing is teaching you about being *a seer.* Your own unique seeing gift and dimension. The Lord says just keep your mouth shut; don't get too verbal about what you are seeing because you are still in the beginning stages of understanding this. So, the Lord says a seeing dimension is going to be well developed in your life in the years ahead.

The Gift Is Activated

The day that I received this word, I began to see things in the spirit around me. I had never had this gifting activated before, and so I was very startled with this new experience. I began to see colors in the spirit, words imposed over the physical things in front of me, body parts randomly appearing, fire or water descending on things, places, or people. I would on occasion even see angels or demons. When I first started seeing these things, I was surprised and even confused. I had to grow, learn, and come into understanding about what was happening. Even now, as I reread the second prophecy from Dennis Cramer, I see such wisdom in his statement, *"The Lord says just keep your mouth shut; don't get too verbal about what you are seeing, because you are still in the beginning stages of understanding this."*

When I first started seeing these things, I was surprised and even confused.

I was really taken aback by this whole new gifting, especially since I didn't have anyone to mentor me in seeing at the time. There are precious few in the Body of Christ who are willing to share their experiences. The Lord had to personally teach me about the things He was showing me.

Flipping the Switch

About a month after Dennis Cramer prophesied over me, the frequency of the visions began to diminish, and again I was confused. I thought, *did I commit some sin that is hindering my seeing ability? Have I done something wrong? What is happening to my gift?*

The Holy Spirit showed me that in the previous month He had sovereignly demonstrated to me the potential of my seer gifting. Now the Lord would teach me how to activate my gifting. In the spirit I saw a large switch, much like a typical wall-mounted light switch. On the switch were the words "On" and "Off," and then in my spirit I heard the meaning. In the first month the Holy Spirit had flipped my switch "On" to enable me to see in the spirit realm around me. Now He was flipping my switch to "Off," and things would be totally normal again. The Holy Spirit told me that He would teach me how to flip the switch myself.

WE MOVE THE SWITCH BY FAITH

With all of the gifts of the Holy Spirit, we have a role in activating them. Sometimes the Holy Spirit will move sovereignly and heal someone, but most of the time faith must be activated. When we read the Gospels, we often see Jesus telling people to take an action—to show themselves to a priest, to wash the mud from their eyes, or to pick up their bed and walk. These were each acts of faith that, when activated, released the gift of healing.

If the Holy Spirit tells me to give a prophetic word, then I must take part in cooperating with the Spirit and deliver the word. When you activate faith, then you have stepped over into the things of the Kingdom realm: healing, prophecy, miracles, discerning of spirits, and so on. The Lord was moving me from relying only on sovereign experiences, into activating my faith to believe for the gift of discerning of spirits to function (see John 5:8; Mark 2:9; John 9:11; Luke 17:11-19).

IN MY EXPERIENCE

From my personal experience I can tell you that when God first opens your spiritual eyes as He did mine, it can be very scary, even terrifying. When it first started, I was not expecting to see into the spirit realm. I wasn't against such experiences—I was just unaware of them.

I would look at a fellow believer and see a background of illuminated light behind him, or I would see a nonbeliever and a darkness or cloud of depression on him. I would see large demonic presences hovering on or above certain buildings. I would see large warrior angels standing guard around certain buildings and churches. There were times I could see angels dancing among us at church during worship. At other times, I would see the worship get cut off by a speaker who was not following the Holy Spirit's leading, and I would see very sad expressions on the angel's faces. It looked as though they were crying because they knew what we were missing out on by worship being cut short. I would see angels carry in strange-looking internal organs that they would put inside of people, and then those same people would later testify to having been healed. I found these experiences overwhelming, and I want to clarify that I didn't read any books that encouraged or directed me in any of this.

Brazil

Six months after Dennis Cramer prophesied into my life, and five months after God began to teach me how I could activate my gifting, the Lord led me into the next level of training.

I took an opportunity to intern for Evangelist Randy Clark for a month in Brazil. While there, I met two seers who greatly encouraged me in my gifting. The first was Pastor Gary Oates. He had traveled with Randy the previous spring and had his own powerful encounter, which activated his spiritual eyes.

His story and experiences are similar to my own, especially in the sense that neither of us were seeking the ability to see—it was something God chose to give us. He is an excellent example of modern seership. God sovereignly opened Gary's eyes in an encounter where Gary had an out-of-body experience, and the Lord took him to Heaven. He writes about this in his book, *Open My Eyes, Lord.*[1]

The second person that I met was one of the foremost worship leaders in Brazil. The Lord has blessed him with a very strong ability to see into the spirit realm. When we met, I asked him to lay hands on me and pray for an increase in my gifting. He was in a hurry to get the worship service started, but he still took a few minutes to pray for me. After he had prayed, he went off to lead worship. The following is what happened to me in that evening worship service.

A Whole New Level

I don't usually respond physically to the Holy Spirit, not because I am unwilling, but I do not easily experience rolling, falling, laughing, or the other manifestations that people have in response to the Holy Spirit. Understanding that about me will help you understand how powerful the following experience was for me.

As worship began, I saw two angels standing on the stage, and they were unlike anything I had ever seen.

As worship began, I saw two angels standing on the stage, and they were unlike anything I had ever seen. They were about 15 feet tall, and there was fire coming out of them—six feet in every direction. I was standing in the front row of the church with Randy, so I was closer to the stage than the rest of the crowd around me when the closest angel began to walk toward me. I wanted to turn and run or get out of his way, but I was unable to move.

He came straight at me and reached out his hand. When he touched my chest, I collapsed to the floor on my side in the fetal position. The spiritual fire from his touch remained on me, causing me to create my own puddle of sweat on the cement floor of the church. In that moment, I began to see more clearly in the spirit than ever before.

The church held about 6,000 people, divided into six sections of chairs. Over each section I saw another angel of fire about the size of a human man, and the fire only emanated out of them about six inches. As the worship intensified I saw more of these smaller angels come down through the ceiling and join the crowd of worshippers. The worship grew so intense that at the height of worship, while the fire angels continued to join in, the crowd looked like a field of grass on fire, an extreme wild fire of worship.

Then I saw a dark cloud over the crowd, and there was lightning flashing across the cloud. I heard two words in my spirit, "New mantle." Randy Clark, knowing that I could see in the spirit, came over to ask me what I was seeing, and I shared with him all that I have written here. Then I asked him to flatten me out on my back because I was in an awkward and uncomfortable position. He flattened me out, and I still did not have control of any of my body below my neck.

While stuck to the ground, I looked down at my body and I saw three angels on me. There was one on each of my legs holding me down with their hands. A third angel was sitting next to me using his right hand to press down on my chest. I could see that the two 15-foot angels of fire were still on the stage watching.

I felt a splash of water come across my chest as if someone had taken a water bottle and poured it on me. I looked around but couldn't figure out who had done it. Then it happened two more times a few minutes later. This felt so real in the natural that I was actually getting annoyed. I didn't understand what this was until later.

Eventually the worship ended, and I was able to make it back to my seat with some help. Later on, I found an interpreter and spoke with the worship leader. I asked him what he had seen that evening, and he told me exactly what I had seen in his own words. He even included that the large angel of fire who had touched me at the beginning had told the worship leader that he was going to step off the stage and minister to me. Also, he saw the three angels lay a mantle over me. It had flames on top and water dripping from the bottom, which is why I had felt the water on my chest and heard in my spirit the words, "New mantle." I had been confused about seeing the dark clouds in the meeting, and then the Lord showed me in His Word about His presence coming in a dark cloud:

"...the mountain burned with fire to the midst of heaven, with darkness, cloud, and thick darkness" (Deuteronomy 4:11 NKJV).

"He made darkness His covering, His canopy around Him—the dark rain clouds of the sky. Out of the brightness of His presence clouds advanced, with hailstones and bolts of lightning" (Psalms 18:11-12).

"Clouds and thick darkness surround Him; righteousness and justice are the foundation of His throne. Fire goes before Him and consumes His foes on every side. His lightning lights up the world; the earth sees and trembles" (Psalms 97:2-4).

Since these experiences in Brazil, I have received this new mantle in my life. The Lord has increased my vision and ability to understand what is happening in the spirit. It is from these experiences that the Lord directed me into my call to teach others about the spirit realm.

ACTIVATION

The Lord taught me about activating my faith and "flipping my switch." In this activation I direct you to prepare your heart for the Lord to teach you about flipping your spiritual switch. As a symbol of activating your faith, I recommend that you anoint yourself with oil. Go to your cupboard or pantry and find some olive or other safe food oil. Take a small dab and place it on yourself—you could put it on your forehead or wherever. As you do this, say this prayer in your own words:

Lord, I receive Your anointing. I desire to grow in my walk with You. I open my heart for more of Your work in and through me. I desire to fulfill the call on my life. I ask for Your anointing to run down upon me now (see Ps. 133).

ENDNOTES

1. Gary Oates, *Open My Eyes, Lord* (Dallas, GA: Open Heaven Publications, 2004).

CHAPTER 2

Spiritual Senses

Because the gift of discerning of spirits is one of the more perplexing gifts, let me clarify some of my language about seeing in the spirit. No believer has the "gift of seeing in the spirit" because there is no such thing. The gift that is actually functioning when someone says that he or she is seeing in the spirit is the gift of discerning of spirits.

Discerning of spirits is a true gift of the Holy Spirit found in First Corinthians 12. The emphasis in this book is seeing in the spirit, which is just one way that discerning of spirits functions. Seers function in a high level of discerning of spirits, usually through spiritual sight. Later I will discuss more about the role of seers in the Church.

DISCERNING OF SPIRITS

The gift of discerning of spirits is a communication gift through which the Holy Spirit makes us aware of our spiritual atmosphere and environment around us. The main way that this functions is through our five spiritual senses that God placed within each of us at creation. To understand how we function in discerning of spirits, we must understand our spiritual senses. Most people only realize that they have five physical senses. The truth is that we have three sets of five senses.

Science has learned that the physical body has five senses that enable us to interact with the environment: taste, touch, smell, sight, and sound. In addition to your five physical senses, every person has five senses in their soul and five senses in their spirit.

May God himself, the God of peace, sanctify you through and through. May your whole spirit, soul and body be kept blameless at the coming of our Lord Jesus Christ (1 Thessalonians 5:23).

Scripture has hundreds of verses that lay out clearly that we are a three-part being consisting of a spirit, soul, and body.

Soul Senses

Experience and culture dictate our own individual reactions to taste, touch, smell, sound, and sight through our soul. For example, *smell* brings back memories. If I were to give flowers to one individual, it may bring back good memories like flowers from a wedding, but if I gave the same flowers to another person, it may bring back bad memories from a funeral. This is not a physical reaction to the flowers or their smell; it is a reaction from the individual soul.

If two people are walking together and they cross the path of a dog, one individual may like dogs and begin to pet the dog; however, the second person may be afraid and begin to feel uncomfortable. This is also a response from the individual soul senses. The way we *see* the world, and the way we *hear* others, is affected by the condition of our soul. Also, the willingness to *touch* certain things like a snake may be easy for some or terrifying for others, depending on the condition of the soul. Even the *taste* of some foods will bring varied responses from different people.

The human soul has senses just like the physical body. Each category of senses has a realm that it interacts with. The physical senses interact with the physical realm, the soul senses interact with the interpersonal realm. And the spirit has senses that interact with the spiritual realm.

Although there are hundreds of books that can help develop the soul or the body, this book is focused on the developing and operating of the spiritual senses.

Spirit Senses

Author and teacher Harold Eberle offers great insight regarding our spiritual senses:

Just as we have five senses that provide us with information about the physical world, we also have senses in touch with the spiritual world. The spiritual senses are just as important as the physical senses. Unfortunately, most of us have not developed our spiritual senses.

Many Christians do not even believe they have any spiritual senses. I like to ask them, "Has the devil ever tempted you?" Of course, they answer yes. Then I like to say, "Well, how did you hear the devil? You could not hear him if you did not have spiritual ears." It is sad, but many people have more faith that the devil talks to us than that God talks to us. In reality, the Bible makes it clear that we all have spiritual eyes and ears.

When Elisha prayed for his servant, he did not pray for God to give him eyes, but he prayed that God would open up his eyes (see 2 Kings 6:17). In Ephesians 1:18, Paul did not pray for the saints to receive eyes, but for God to open the eyes of their hearts. We already have spiritual eyes and ears. What we need is to have them opened. We need to become sensitive.[1]

It is a fact that we have senses in our spirit through which we interact with the spirit realm. When the gift of discerning of spirits is functioning, it is through these spiritual senses that we receive communication.

In human communication, the two main senses we use most often for relating information are sound and sight. Communication in the natural is received through listening, as well as through body language and facial expressions. God also communicates through the other three senses (taste, touch, and smell), but most of the time He will speak through seeing and hearing. Because the spiritual senses of taste, smell, and touch are the least understood, the following examples show how, on occasion, God may speak to us through these senses.

Communication in the natural is received through listening, as well as through body language and facial expressions.

TASTE

And He said to me, "Son of man, eat what is before you, eat this scroll; then go and speak to the house of Israel." So I opened my mouth, and He gave me the scroll to eat. Then He said to me, "Son of man, eat this scroll I am giving you and fill your stomach with it." So I ate it, and it tasted as sweet as honey in my mouth" (Ezekiel 3:1-3).

If we suddenly taste something sweet, sour, or salty, but the taste is not a result of anything we have physically had to eat or drink, we should ask the Lord if He is trying to speak to us. On occasion, in the Old Testament, God spoke to His prophets through experiences with spiritual taste.

SMELL

But thanks be to God, who always leads us in triumphal procession in Christ and through us, spreads everywhere the fragrance of the knowledge of Him (2 Corinthians 2:14).

In the spring of 2005 I was helping Randy Clark and Leif Hetland at one of their book tables in Nashville, Tennessee, when a large angel appeared at the end of the table by Leif's books, and a stir began among the people. To my knowledge, no one else was able to see what I was seeing, yet they could smell the change. I saw the angel pulling out small vials of heavenly fragrances, each one being very distinct. He pulled them from his belt and wafted them in the air. There was the scent of perfect cinnamon; then after about two minutes, a fresh scent would be put out. The scents were drastically different from one another: from the scent of cinnamon to wild flowers to baby oil and then to various spices. This continued through about 12 different smells, and by the end of 30 minutes there were about 30 people crowded together on the tips of their toes smelling the air and sharing in the experience.

TOUCH

As Jesus was on His way, the crowds almost crushed Him. And a woman was there who had been subject to bleeding for 12 years, but no one could heal her. She came up behind Him and touched the edge of His cloak, and immediately her bleeding stopped. "Who touched Me?" Jesus asked. When they all denied it, Peter said, "Master, the people are crowding and pressing against You." But Jesus said, "Someone touched Me; I know that power has gone out from Me" (Luke 8:43-46).

This is a great example of the difference between physical touch and spiritual touch. According to this story, Jesus was almost physically crushed, but when someone reached out and drew healing power out from His spirit, He declared that someone had touched Him, speaking spiritually, of course.

My friend Benjamin Valence and I had a spiritual experience together a few years ago. Ben wrote out the experience in his own words as he remembers it (notice how the senses of touch and smell were both operating).

I reached out my hands and began to feel what was there

I remember it like it was yesterday. Jonathan and I were sitting in his kitchen talking about things of the spirit when we stepped into some activation. As we were talking about angels and things of the unseen realm, Jonathan suddenly told me there was something in front of me (in the spirit) on the table and that I should reach out my hands to feel what it was. To most this might seem a little weird, but he and I had been operating in discerning of spirits for quite a while, so I didn't hesitate. I reached out my hands and began to feel what was there; I could make out something that felt like a large bowl. It felt as real as if I was feeling a bowl in the natural realm. As I was telling Jonathan what I felt, he would confirm it by seeing in the spirit what I was touching. He would then ask me what else I felt, always trying to get me to reach a little deeper. As I felt out the bowl Jon asked me to feel inside of it, and as I reached into the bowl I could literally feel a hot liquid on my hand. After realizing I could feel heat coming from the bowl when I placed my hands inside it, I tried putting my face over it. As soon as I did, my face became hot, and I began to sweat; it was incredible. After a while of playing with the bowl, Jon told me that it was oil and asked me to pick it up and to pour it over my head. As soon as I reached for the bowl and began to tilt it over my head, Jon and I looked at each other, and as if repeating each other's words said, "Did you smell that?" At the same moment we both smelled the scent of oil fill the room. Excitement boiled inside me as I raised the bowl over my head and began to pour it out. I could actually feel the oil running down over my head and heat coming from the substance. I will never forget the feeling of the oil running over me as if consuming my senses. I felt peace, joy, and love of the Father washing over me. I will never forget that day.

FOCUS ON THE LORD

Once I started to share what I was able to see, people were very hungry to have similar experiences and would ask me how they could begin to see. Since God had sovereignly given me this gift that I had not sought out, I didn't know what to tell them, until I found a key in Matthew 5:8.

I understood impartation through the laying on of hands; therefore I would pray for impartation to anyone interested, but I was only seeing a fraction of people receive the gifting. (I will address impartation in greater detail in a later chapter.) Over the last several years, the Lord has taught me some principles that have opened the door for more people to be able to activate their faith for the gift of discerning of spirits. The first one that I want to share is the principle of Matthew 5:8, which was the first insight the Lord gave me: *Blessed are the pure in heart for they shall see God* (Matt. 5:8).

How pure does a person have to be to see God? I believe that the answer is in asking the right question, "What is meant by purity?" The vast majority of believers hold the word *pure* as a moral standard that is unattainable. Jesus was speaking of purity as a key to seeing God and I believe He told us this because it is attainable.

To illustrate the meaning of *pure*, take gold as an example. When gold has been truly purified, it has had all the other elements removed from it. This process causes all the dross and impurities to come to the surface so it can be skimmed away. In the end, it produces gold that is one single element. Our hearts are sometimes cluttered with the dross of life, and we must remove all the distractions so we can focus our whole heart on God. For us to have a "pure" heart, our heart must be focused. If we are to "see God," then the one element our heart contains must be a focus on the Lord.

When we focus our hearts on the Lord, we are aimed to come into the experience of seeing God. The verse is clearer if we read it this way, "Happy are those who focus their heart on God, for they will actually see God."

Faith and the Empty Chair

The following story is a favorite of mine. It is a great illustration of what it means to focus your heart on Jesus using the eyes of your imagination.

A man's daughter had asked the local minister to come and pray with her father. When the minister arrived, he found the man lying in bed with his head propped up on two pillows. An empty chair sat beside his bed. The minister assumed that the old man had been informed of his impending visit. "I guess you were expecting me," he said. "No, who are you?" said the father. "I'm the new minister at your church," he replied. "When I saw the empty chair, I figured you knew I was going to show up."

"Oh yeah, the chair," said the bedridden man. "Would you mind closing the door?" Puzzled, the minister shut the door. "I have never told anyone this, not even my daughter," said the man. "But all of my life I have never known how to pray. At church I used to hear the preacher talk about prayer, but it went right over my head."

It's not spooky because He promised, "I'll be with you always."

"I abandoned any attempt at prayer," the old man continued, "until one day about four years ago my best friend said to me, 'Joe, prayer is just a simple matter of having a conversation with Jesus. Here is what I suggest. Sit down in a chair; place an empty chair in front of you, and, in faith, see Jesus in the chair. It's not spooky because He promised, "I'll be with you always." Then just speak to Him and listen in the same way you're doing with me right now.'"

"So, I tried it and I've liked it so much that I do it a couple of hours every day. I'm careful though. If my daughter saw me talking to an empty chair, she'd either have a nervous breakdown or send me off to the funny farm."

The minister was deeply moved by the story and encouraged the old man to continue on the journey. Then he prayed with him and returned to the church building. Two nights later the daughter called to tell the minister that her daddy had died that afternoon. "Did he die in peace?" he asked.

"Yes, when I left the house about two o'clock, he called me over to his bedside, told me he loved me, and kissed me on the cheek. When I got back from the store an hour later, I found him dead. But there was something strange about his death. Apparently, just before Daddy died, he leaned over and rested his head on the chair beside the bed. What do you make of that?" The minister wiped a tear from his eye and said, "I wish we all could go that way."

ACTIVATION I

For the first exercise we are going to talk to Jesus like the old man in the story did. First put in your bookmark and set the book down, then close your eyes and with your imagination, picture Jesus.

Now engage in a conversation with Him. If you cannot think of anything to say, you can always start by thanking Him for the things He has done in your life. For example, salvation, physical healing, emotional freedom, baptism in the Holy Spirit, financial blessing, reconciliation with others, divine favor, deliverance, and the fruit and gifts of the Spirit. Do not forget to listen to the Lord speaking back to you.

ACTIVATION II

For the second activation, you are going to pray a simple prayer, consecrating your senses to the Lord.

Do not offer the parts of your body to sin, as instruments of wickedness, but rather offer yourselves to God, as those who have been brought from death to life; and offer the parts of your body to Him as instruments of righteousness (Romans 6:13).

Pray this prayer of offering in your own words:

Lord,

I offer to You all the parts of my body including my spiritual senses. My spiritual ability to see, hear, taste, smell, and touch I give to You alone. I offer myself to You as an instrument of righteousness.

ENDNOTES

1. Harold Eberle, Partnership Newsletter (Yakima, WA: Worldcast Ministries, May 2008).

CHAPTER 3

Impartation

To understand impartation, you have to understand anointing, which in the Bible means "a smearing." In Scripture, oil is symbolic of the Holy Spirit. When a prophet or priest poured, rubbed, or smeared oil over the head of someone, it was referred to as anointing that person. This actually gave the anointed person a measure of the oil that belonged to the prophet or priest. This is commonly referred to as transferring the anointing.

In the Old Testament, the oil was used to signify the passing of the anointing. In the New Testament we find that the anointing of the Holy Spirit can now be passed through the laying on of hands because the anointing abides within us: *"But the anointing which you have received from Him abides in you..."* (1 John 2:27).

IMPARTATION IS FOUNDATIONAL

The apostle Paul named the laying on of hands as one of the six basic fundamental doctrines a Christian should understand. This places it in the very foundation of our Christian beliefs. In many circles of the modern Church, impartation is ignored, if not denied all together; in the first century, it was considered a foundational truth:

> *Therefore let us leave the elementary doctrines about Christ and go on to maturity, not laying again the foundation of...the laying on of hands...* (Hebrews 6:1-2).

Paul also thought of impartation as part of the process of becoming established. He imparted spiritual gifts to the Roman believers to give them a better foundation: "For I long to see you, that I may impart to you some spiritual gift, so that you may be established..." (Rom. 1:11 NKJV).

Impartation Is Intentional

In the Old Testament, the anointing was a very purposeful, pronounced event. Impartation occurs not just because of touch, but because a person places his or her hands on you by the direction of the Holy Spirit with a goal in mind. Intentionally, the impartation occurs.

To say that impartation occurs every time touch occurs would be similar to saying that if an Old Testament prophet had a leaky oil flask, then everything that he dripped oil on was anointed to be king. If it were just touch, then every time you shook someone's hand, you would have some of him or her rub off on you. This is not biblical, and we are not promoting such superstition. We intentionally give that which we have, by the direction of the Holy Spirit: *"what I have I give you..."* (Acts 3:6).

Impartation Is Biblical

There are many other examples throughout the Bible of individuals or groups of people receiving an impartation from the Lord through another person. Let's look at a few of these.

Joshua and Moses: *Now Joshua the son of Nun was full of the spirit of wisdom, for Moses had laid his hands on him; so the children of Israel heeded him, and did as the Lord had commanded Moses* (Deut. 34:9 NKJV).

Moses and the Elders: *So Moses went out and told the people the words of the Lord, and he gathered the seventy men of the elders of the people and placed them around the tabernacle. Then the Lord came down in the cloud, and spoke to him, and took of the Spirit that was upon him, and placed the same upon the seventy elders; and it happened, when the Spirit rested upon them, that they prophesied...* (Num. 11:24-25a NKJV).

Elijah and Elisha: *And so it was, when they had crossed over, that Elijah said to Elisha, "Ask! What may I do for you, before I am taken away from you?" Elisha said, "Please let a double portion of your spirit be upon me"* (2 Kings 2:9 NKJV).

Peter: *Then Peter said, "Silver and gold I do not have, but what I do have I give you: In the name of Jesus Christ of Nazareth, rise up and walk"* (Acts 3:6 NKJV).

Paul and Timothy: *Do not neglect the gift that is in you, which was given to you by prophecy with the laying on of the hands of the eldership* (1 Tim. 4:14).

Timothy was deeply impacted by impartation. Specifically, as a result of impartation, he received a spiritual gift through the laying on of hands and prophecy by a prophetic presbytery of elders: *"Therefore I remind you to stir up the gift of God which is in you through the laying on of my hands"* (2 Tim. 1:6 NKJV).

IMPARTATION IS INDIVIDUAL

Does everyone receive the same level of impartation when hands are laid on? Some have thought that if a famous Christian leader lays his or her hands on an individual, then the receiver will get an impartation that instantly gives them an equal portion of the anointing.

Our character must be able to uphold the amount of power we carry.

It is the mercy of God that protects us from receiving more than we can handle. As Pastor Bill Johnson of Redding, California, says, "Revelation always brings responsibility, and hunger is the thing that prepares our hearts to carry the weight of that responsibility."[1] Our character must be able to uphold the amount of power we carry, or else we are a danger to those around us. So the answer is no, not everyone receives the same level of anointing in impartation. God knows what you need, and what you can handle.

IMPARTATION IS A SEED, NOT A FULL-GROWN PLANT

The parable of the sower (see Luke 8:4-15) teaches us how the farmer spreads the seeds for salvation, and it also teaches us a principle of how we receive from God. Our heart is the soil, and Father God is the farmer who spreads seed, which is the Word of God (or, for our analogy, impartation). He casts it into the soil of our heart. Then the birds, which are demonic attacks, come to kill, steal, and destroy.

This is where the variation in impartation can occur. The difference in how any seed grows depends on the soil in which it is planted and how prepared and ready that soil is for seeds to grow. After the seed is planted, it can grow very quickly if it is given the proper water (time in the presence of the Holy Spirit—see John 7:38-39) and sunlight (Jesus is the light that the seed needs to grow—see 2 Cor. 4:4).

To my knowledge, those who have some of the most powerful impartations are among the following: those who are hungry for more of God, pastors who are tired and burned out, and people whose ministry is desperate for a breakthrough. They are people whose soil is eager for seed, and almost as soon as the seed hits the soil, something sprouts. The soil is already prepared with water and sunlight, but the impartation is needed to move into producing. In contrast, there are those who have no hunger for God, do not spend time with the Holy Spirit, and do not walk in the light of Christ, leaving their hearts as hard as rocky soil. Usually, God has to plow this ground before any seed can grow there.

One other factor in farming is the needed pressure that dirt places against a seed so that the shell cracks open and the seed can begin to grow. Seeds that have never sprouted, because they have never been planted in dirt, have been found in the tombs of pharaohs. Some of these seeds, which are over 4,000 years old, have since been planted in dirt and have sprouted and produced. That is why seeds of salvation can be tossed out on the ground of peoples' hearts day after day with no results, but when the trials of life give the needed pressure, the seeds crack open and life sprouts.

This pressure comes into the impartation discussion because not only spiritually hungry people get powerful impartation. Sometimes it is a person about to lose his or her ministry, or someone about to give up from difficulty. Someone under tremendous pressure in life may be the most ready for the seed of impartation to be planted in his or her heart.

YOU CAN ONLY IMPART WHAT YOU POSSESS

It is crucial that we understand this next point: you can only impart what you possess—if you possess it, you can impart it. If you don't have it, don't lay hands on another and declare impartation. If you only have olive anointing oil in your flask, you can't declare and impart cedar anointing oil to someone else. Yes, pray that God would give it to them. But don't go claiming to impart what you don't have in your own life. You cannot impart resurrection power to someone if you have never raised the dead, but you can declare and prophesy it over someone if the Lord directs you.

"The double portion," as it relates to impartation, is a phrase commonly heard in some church circles. To understand the double portion correctly, consider the following scenario. If an Old Testament prophet was sent to anoint a king and the prophet has ten ounces of anointing oil in his flask, he can only give the king ten ounces. If the king asks him to give him a double portion of all the anointing that the prophet had, this would mean that he wanted not 10 ounces, but 20 ounces. He cannot give 20 because he only has 10. That is double the portion of all the anointing that the prophet has. This is what Elisha did when he asked for a double portion of Elijah's anointing. Elijah responded by saying, *"You have asked a difficult thing"* (2 Kings 2:10a). Then, because an individual does not have the ability to give a double portion to another person, Elijah puts the responsibility on God by saying, *"If you see me when I am taken from you, it will be yours—otherwise not"* (2 Kings 2:10b). This is a proper understanding of the concept of the double portion referred to by Elisha. Notice that even the prophet Elijah was not able to freely give away the double portion; he responded, in essence, that God would have to do it. It may prove wise to use this term with a little more caution.

First Timothy 5:22 raises another important question regarding the practice of impartation: *"Do not be hasty in the laying on of hands, and do not share in the sins of others. Keep yourself pure."* If pulled out of its original context, this verse can seem very contradictory to everything I have presented in this chapter. A large part of First Timothy is written about setting church leadership into positions of author-ity. All of chapter 3 lays out detailed qualifications about what type of person is to be put into leadership. A few verses earlier, Paul writes, *"The elders who direct the affairs of the church well are worthy of double honor, especially those whose work is preaching and teaching. For the Scripture says, 'Do not muzzle the ox while it is tread-ing out the grain,' and 'The worker deserves his wages.' Do not entertain an accusation against an elder unless it is brought by two or three witnesses. Those who sin are to be rebuked publicly, so that the others may take warning"* (1 Tim. 5:17-20).

Transference of the anointing by the laying on of hands for impartation...exists to help you grow.

In First Timothy, Paul is writing about the laying on of hands for setting leadership into positions of authority. This has nothing to do with the concept of impartation. It would not make sense for Paul to write in Hebrews 6 and Romans 1 that he wanted to lay hands on baby Christians that *"they may be established"*

(Rom. 1:11), and then to warn in First Timothy that you can share in the sins of others by laying hands on them. If he is referring to the same type of laying on of hands in both passages, then wouldn't he say to "keep yourself pure" by not laying hands on people who are not yet "established" (1 Tim. 5:22; Rom. 1:11)? There are two different types of laying on of hands: one for setting leaders into places of authority, and the second for imparting and transferring anointing. There are qualifications and restrictions on the first type, but the second type actually propels you toward being qualified. Transference of the anointing by the laying on of hands for impartation is for each and every Christian and is not held back; in fact, it exists to help you grow.

ACTIVATION

There are many Scripture verses that validate the fact that impartation can occur through the touching of physical objects (see Matt. 9:20; 14:35-37; Acts 19:11-12). The exercise for this chapter will be a prayer for receiving impartation. Place one hand on this book, while placing your other hand on yourself. Put this prayer in your own words and stir up your faith:

> I receive an impartation right now from the Holy Spirit for an increase in discerning of spirits. I receive anointing for my eyes to see (see Rev. 3:18), I receive an impartation for the eyes of my understanding to be enlightened (see Eph. 1:17-18), and I receive an impartation for greater vision in the spirit realm.

ENDNOTE

1. Bill Johnson, *Dreaming With God* (Shippensburg, PA: Destiny Image, 2006), 60.

CHAPTER 4

We Can All See

You Can Learn

Many people do not understand that spiritual gifts can be taught. The apostle Paul said that he didn't want us to be ignorant about the spiritual gifts (see 1 Cor. 12:1), and what corrects ignorance better than teaching?

Some say that Paul was only referring to teaching about the gifts in a general sense rather than activating the gifts as in a classroom setting. If Paul was against the idea of activations so that all may learn, then why would he say, *"For you can all prophesy one by one, that all may learn and all may be encouraged"* (see 1 Cor. 14:31 NKJV)?

The gifts can be taught, learned, and activated.

The gifts can be taught, learned, and activated. Paul also set a precedent by encouraging his spiritual son, Timothy, to activate his gifting: *"Therefore I remind you to stir up the gift of God which is in you through the laying on of my hands"* (2 Tim. 1:6). I believe that this charge applies to us as well; we are to activate our giftings, not merely to wait and hope that the Holy Spirit will cause our gift to activate: *"But solid food belongs to those who are of full age, that is, those who by reason of use have their senses exercised to discern both good and evil"* (Heb. 5:14).

How Many Gifts Do I Have?

Many have been taught that they only have access to one (possibly more but not all) of the gifts of the Holy Spirit. This teaching has limited the operation of the Holy Spirit in the Church because believers will not step out in faith to use a gift, since it might not be "their gift." When they do not step out, they do not find out what their gifting is, and satan has effectively immobilized the use of the spiritual gifts.

There are two main verses that have been misunderstood and misapplied, and this has caused most of the confusion surrounding the spiritual gifts. These verses seem to say that we as individuals have a limited access to the gifts that have been given to the Church.

But the manifestation of the Spirit is given to each one for the profit of all...distributing to each one individually as He wills (1 Corinthians 12:7-11 NKJV).

As each one has received a gift, minister it to one another, as good stewards of the manifold grace of God (1 Peter 4:10 NKJV).

There is a teaching that expands on First Peter 4:10, stating that each Christian has been given only one gift (possibly two or three but not more), and this gift is resident within the individual and can be called on at any time. First Corinthians 12:11 also seems to be in agreement with this concept. I agree with this teaching, but only when it is balanced by a seemingly contradictory idea.

THE FAITH LEVEL OF OPERATION

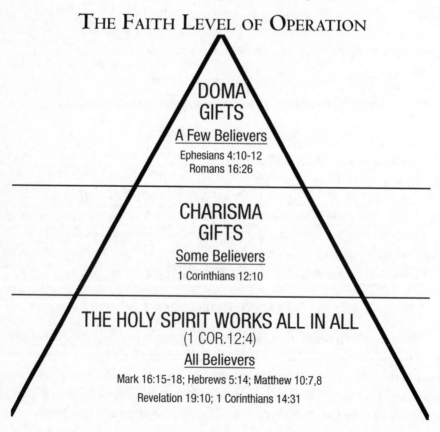

DOMA
GIFTS
A Few Believers
Ephesians 4:10-12
Romans 16:26

CHARISMA
GIFTS
Some Believers
1 Corinthians 12:10

THE HOLY SPIRIT WORKS ALL IN ALL
(1 COR.12:4)
All Believers
Mark 16:15-18; Hebrews 5:14; Matthew 10:7,8
Revelation 19:10; 1 Corinthians 14:31

Although First Corinthians 12 gives us a list of nine spiritual gifts and says that the Holy Spirit distributes to each one individually as He wills, we find what seems to be a contradiction. It also says of the gifts that "...*God works all in all*" (1 Cor. 12:6). How can the Holy Spirit give you a gift, uniquely yours, if He also gives everyone that same gift?

Another seeming contradiction is prophecy. It appears on our list of nine special gifts given to individuals, yet we read, "*For you can all prophesy...*" (1 Cor. 14:31).

And what about the gift of healing? Is it a gift that only some have, or should we all lay our hands on the sick and see healing? As Mark 16:17-18 says, "*And these signs will accompany those who believe: ...they will place their hands on sick people, and they will get well.*" If I don't have the gift of healing available to me, how could I be responsible for not praying for the sick? Yet I am commanded to heal the sick in Matthew 10:8: "*Heal the sick, raise the dead, cleanse those who have leprosy, drive out demons. Freely you have received, freely give.*" How can God be "just" if He commands me to do something for which He has not equipped me?

Lastly, what about discerning of spirits? Hebrews 5:14 says, "But solid food belongs to those who are of full age, that is, those **who by reason of use have their senses exercised to discern** both good and evil." But if only some Christians have been given the gift of discerning of spirits, then how can God ask that we all discern good from evil?

THREE DIFFERENT LEVELS IN THE GIFTS

The missing piece here is that there are three different levels of the spiritual gifts. Take prophecy, for example: On the highest level you have the office of the prophet mentioned in Ephesians 4:11-13; on the middle level is the gift of prophecy found in First Corinthians 12:10; and on the lowest level is the faith level where Paul says, "*you can all prophesy*" (1 Cor. 14:31). The progression works like a triangle; at the bottom, everyone can prophesy; as you move to the middle of the triangle, some people will have the actual gift of prophecy; lastly, there will be a few people at the top of the triangle who have the calling of a prophet. Just because you can prophesy does not mean you have the gift of prophecy, and just because you have the gift of prophecy does not mean that you have the office and calling of a prophet.

Let us take the triangle of three levels and apply it to discernment. On the top of the triangle we find the office of the seer; at the middle there is the gift of discerning of spirits; and at the bottom we have the faith level referred to in Hebrews 5:14: *"those who are of full age, that is, those who by reason of use have their senses exercised to discern both good and evil."* As with prophecy, just because you can discern does not mean that you have the gift of discerning of spirits, and even if you can see in the spirit and have the gift of discerning of spirits, this does not mean that you are in the office and calling of a seer. Many have operated in the lower two levels and have declared themselves to be prophets and seers in the Body of Christ, and this has brought much unnecessary spiritual warfare against them. It is spiritually dangerous to declare that you are a prophet or a seer unless you truly are one. A surefire way to know if you are a prophet or a seer is to look at the one passage that gives the New Testament job description of a true prophet: *"And He Himself gave some to be apostles, some prophets, some evangelists, and some pastors and teachers, for the equipping of the saints for the work of ministry, for the edifying of the body of Christ"* (Eph. 4:11-12 NKJV). The New Testament prophet is supposed to be equipping others for the work of ministry; if you are not equipping others in prophecy, then you are probably not a prophet.

"HAVING EYES, DO YOU NOT SEE?" (MARK 8:18)

Many verses in the Bible state that all Christians can and should have their spiritual eyes and ears open and functioning. We often pass over clear references to spiritual sight because we have been told that seeing in the spirit is not our gift. Here is a quick overview of seven sections of Scripture that speak of how every believer should have their spiritual eyes operating.

We often pass over clear references to spiritual sight because we have been told that seeing in the spirit is not our gift.

---

1. Hebrews 5:12-14: *"For though by this time you ought to be teachers, you need someone to teach you again the first principles of the oracles of God; and you have come to need milk and not solid food. For everyone who partakes only of milk is unskilled in the word of righteousness, for he is a babe. But solid food belongs to those who are of full age, that is, those who by reason of use have their senses exercised to discern both good and evil"* (NKJV).

We Can All See

This shows that a sign of all mature Christians is that they will be active in using discernment. This is not only available to us, but it is also a sign of maturity. It is time to grow and start using our discernment.

2. Ephesians 1:15-18: *"Therefore I also, after I heard of your faith in the Lord Jesus and your love for all the saints, do not cease to give thanks for you, making mention of you in my prayers: that the God of our Lord Jesus Christ, the Father of glory, may give to you the spirit of wisdom and revelation in the knowledge of Him, the eyes of your understanding being enlightened; that you may know what is the hope of His calling, what are the riches of the glory of His inheritance in the saints"* (NKJV).

If Paul believed that only certain Christians could see in the spirit, then why would he be wasting his time praying for all the Ephesian believers to have the eyes of their understanding enlightened? Obviously, Paul believed that all of them could have their spiritual eyes opened.

3. Second Kings 6:15-17: *"And when the servant of the man of God arose early and went out, there was an army, surrounding the city with horses and chariots. And his servant said to him, "Alas, my master! What shall we do?" So he answered, "Do not fear, for those who are with us are more than those who are with them." And Elisha prayed, and said, "Lord, I pray, open his eyes that he may see." Then the Lord opened the eyes of the young man, and he saw. And behold, the mountain was full of horses and chariots of fire all around Elisha"* (NKJV).

Elisha didn't pray, "If it is my servant's gifting, open his eyes." No, Elisha knew that God wanted to open the eyes of the servant, as God always wants to open the eyes of His servants. There is no question that God has given us all spiritual eyes that would have worked perfectly before the Fall of Adam—why shouldn't they work in every born-again believer?

Elisha knew that God wanted to open the eyes of the servant

---

4. Revelation 3:17-18: *"Because you say, 'I am rich, have become wealthy, and have need of nothing'—and do not know that you are wretched, miserable, poor, blind, and naked—I counsel you to buy from Me gold refined in the fire, that you may be rich; and white garments, that you may be clothed, that the shame of your nakedness may not be revealed; and anoint your eyes with eye salve, that you may see"* (NKJV).

Spiritually we are poor and naked, and God wants to spiritually clothe us and give us spiritual riches. But the third part of the verse still causes offense to some—that we are blind and that God wants us to anoint our eyes with eye salve so that we may see. But we are spiritually blind, and God has provided an anointing that can open the spiritual eyes of every believer. God has not excluded even one person by limiting His gifts to only a few. This anointing of Revelation 3 is available to all, as is the clothing and gold that He has provided for us.

5. Luke 4:18: *"The Spirit of the Lord is on Me, because He has anointed Me to preach good news to the poor. He has sent Me to proclaim freedom for the prisoners and recovery of sight for the blind, to release the oppressed..."*

This verse is rarely thought of as referring to spiritual sight, but let us look a little closer. Jesus said that He was anointed to preach good news to the poor, which is a spiritual activity. He was anointed to proclaim freedom to the prisoners and to release the oppressed. I propose that this does not refer to actual prisoners and oppressed people, as evidenced by the fact that Jesus was not literally opening jail cells to set captives free. Instead, He healed and freed hearts and delivered others of demonic oppression. This leads to the conclusion that perhaps Jesus was not only healing the physically blind, which He certainly did, but also the spiritually blind.

6. Matthew 7:1-5: *"Do not judge or you too will be judged. For in the same way you judge others, you will be judged, and with the measure you use, it will be measured to you. Why do you look at the speck of sawdust in your brother's eye and pay no attention to the plank in your own eye? How can you say to your brother, "Let me take the speck out of your eye," when all the time there is a plank in your own eye? You hypocrite, first take the plank out of your own eye, and then you will see clearly to remove the speck from your brother's eye."*

Clearly Jesus, using metaphor and hyperbole (exaggeration to make a point), is not speaking of the physical eye. He is speaking of how we see the world through the eyes of our heart, and how at times we get a speck or a log that hinders our seeing. This also speaks of how hypocrisy operates.

7. First John 2:9-11: *"Anyone who claims to be in the light but hates his brother is still in the darkness. Whoever loves his brother lives in the light, and there is nothing in him to make him stumble. But whoever hates his brother is in the darkness and walks around in the darkness; he does not know where he is going, because the darkness has blinded his eyes."*

When a Christian hates another believer, does that Christian go physically blind? Of course not! This is speaking of how hate blinds our spiritual eyes. We must operate our discernment through love. Hate hinders, obscures, and destroys Christ-like discernment.

AN OPEN HEART

The issue of who has what gifts and how many one person can operate in has been the topic of much debate in certain church circles. I hope this quick overview of seven examples of God's desire for every person to operate in spiritual sight has helped to open your heart and your mind. There is so much more available to us, and we must remain open to finding new truth in the Word. We should heed what the apostle Paul said and *"...eagerly desire the greater gifts"* (1 Cor. 12:31). Now that we understand the levels among the gifts, we can truly pursue greater gifts.

We must remain open to finding new truth in the Word.

ACTIVATION

The words *revelation, interpretation,* and *application* can serve as a simple and straightforward way to process information from the spirit realm. First, God shows you something . Second, you ask the Lord, what the revelation means. Third, ask the Lord what you should do with the information that He just gave you.

Revelation: Ask the Lord to show you a picture in your imagination.

Interpretation: Ask the Lord what the picture means.

Application: Ask the Lord what you should do in response. Perhaps you should just receive the picture and be encouraged, but He may say that the picture is for someone else and that you should encourage that person with what He showed you.

Write out in your journal the revelation and the interpretation and application, this will keep the revelation for future encouragement. These three steps can be remembered as the acronym R.I.A. and can be applied to any vision, dream, or picture from the Lord.

CHAPTER 5

Prophets and Seers

The question that I get asked the most is, "What is a seer?" The response I give is different, depending on who is asking. There are three general categories of people who ask this question, and I answer according to which group they are a part of.

If the person asking is not a Christian, then I cannot use Christian lingo to explain it. I use terms they might understand and mold my answer to make sense to them. I might respond by saying, "A person who operates as a seer can see into the spirit realm around us, similar to a psychic person. The difference is that a Christian has legal access to operate in that realm because Jesus lives inside of a Christian. A psychic has no right to operate in that realm, and it is dangerous for them to do so. God communicates to seers through visions, open visions, and dreams, as well as many other ways."

God communicates to seers through visions, open visions, and dreams, as well as many other ways."

If the person is a Christian, but they have no familiarity with prophets and prophecy, then I would probably say something like, "Remember how in the Old Testament Samuel would have visions and speak God's Word to others? Well, that is what a seer and a prophet do. God talks to seers and prophets in different ways; then they take those messages and declare them to the Church to bring vision, direction, and encouragement."

When a person who is very familiar with prophets and prophecy asks, "What is a seer?" there are usually a few other questions implied. The implied questions are various: "Does it matter that we distinguish between seers and prophets?" "Are seers in the New Testament?" "Who are the seers in the Bible?" and "How are prophets and seers different?" Since the previous two groups have just been answered, I will answer these questions in more detail.

Q: Does it Matter That We Distinguish Between Seers and Prophets?

A: The Bible is our example. If it is important to God, then it should be important to us. Scripture is not arbitrary in the use of the titles *seer* and *prophet*. Individuals were referred to as one or the other. This was not a synonymous term that was thrown around interchangeably. Here is an example of Scripture very specifically separating the two terms: *"As for the events of King David's reign, from beginning to end, they are written in the records of Samuel the seer, the records of Nathan the prophet and the records of Gad the seer..."* (1 Chron. 29:29). God clearly distinguished between Samuel and Gad as seers and Nathan as a prophet. If it is important to God, then it should be important to us.

Q: Who Are the Seers in the Bible?

A: There are nine people identified as seers in the Old Testament. There are many others who operated at times in the gifting of a seer such as Balaam, Elisha, Daniel, and Zechariah, but they were never given the title of "seer" in the Bible. Only nine people have been given the name, title, and calling of seer. Listed here are the nine, the scriptural reference of their title as a seer, and the main position that they fulfilled.

Samuel	1 Chronicles 29:29	Governmental advisor
Gad	1 Chronicles 29:29	Governmental advisor
Zadok	2 Samuel 15:27	Chief priest
Hanani	2 Chronicles 16:7	Grandson of Samuel
Iddo	2 Chronicles 9:29	Priest
Amos	Amos 7:12	Sycamore fig picker, marketplace minister
Asaph	2 Chronicles 29:30	Worship leader, author of Psalms 50 and 73-83
Jeduthun	2 Chronicles 35:15	Worship leader
Heman	1 Chronicles 25:5	Worship leader, author of Psalm 88

Take note of the positions that the seers fulfilled. One-third of them were governmental or marketplace oriented, one-third of them were worship leaders, and one-fourth were in formal priesthood ministry. Also we can see from Hanani that the seer anointing can be passed generationally. Many times the title of seer is applied to others such as Ezekiel and Elisha, but these nine are the only ones in the entire Bible who God refers to as seers.

Q: Are There Seers in the New Testament?

A: According to First Samuel 9:9, *"Formerly in Israel, when a man went to inquire of God, he spoke thus: 'Come, let us go to the seer'; for he who is now called a prophet was formerly called a seer."* In our modern day we can lose the history and context behind biblical words. This verse shows us that in the progression of the Hebrew language; they blended the word seer into the word *prophet* and called them the same thing. A prophet and a seer refer to the same calling, yet the way that they receive their revelation from the Lord functions differently. The seers continued to minister in Israel, so this was not a dismissal of seers but merely a change in language trends. This is similar to the fact that there are electrical engineers, mechanical engineers, civil engineers, and many other kinds, with a world of difference between them, but for convenience we just say engineer.

When we read the New Testament, we find no reference to the word *seers*. This is because the first-century reader understood that the word *prophet* was inclusive of both prophets and seers. (If First Samuel 9:9 had eliminated the use of the term *prophet* in favor of the word *seer*, then we would still have five New Testament offices listed in Ephesians 4:11, but prophet would be included under seer). When first-century believers read the words of Paul in Ephesians 4:11, they technically saw six ministries, not just five: *"It was He who gave some to be apostles, some to be prophets* [the word *prophet* is inclusive of seers]*, some to be evangelists, and some to be pastors and teachers"* (Eph. 4:11). Seers and prophets still both exist, and they are both called to deliver the prophetic word of the Lord, but they function differently (more on that later).

Q: How Are Prophets and Seers Different?

A1: A simple way to determine whether someone is a prophet or a seer in the Bible is to watch for the prophetic prefix they use. If, when they prophesy, they say, "The Lord would say," then it is likely they are hearing the word of the Lord bubble up inside of them as a prophet. The root word for prophet is *nabi*. Dennis Cramer gives a great explanation of what *nabi* means:

> The Hebrew word for *prophet* (occurring 300 times in the Old Testament) means a suddenly inspired person. The word implies one who bubbles up, one who flows forth. Some might call this biblical phenomenon *prophetic effervescence*—the sudden bubbling up or flowing forth of the prophetic message from deep within the human spirit. Many prophetic believers, whether they are prophets or merely prophetic, will experience this type of prophesying. "Nabi" style prophecy is a spontaneous bubbling up, a sudden inspiration to prophesy with little or no foreknowledge.[1]

A2: A seer would more often say, "The Lord showed me," or "it was likened unto," or "I saw," and then an explanation would follow. Paula Price, the author of *The Prophet's Dictionary* writes of seers,

> The Hebrew word for seer is one who receives communications from God more from visions and dreams than audible words. Prophets who say they saw the word of the Lord more than heard it is an example of this type of prophet.[2]

Well-known prophetic author Cindy Jacobs writes in her book *The Voice of God*,

> Prophets in the Old Testament at one time were called "seers." This means that they literally or figuratively saw things in the Spirit. Some of the prophets were more pictorial in their gifts than others, such as Ezekiel who saw visions of heavenly creatures. Certain prophetic people today receive their prophetic words mainly through pictures. Their prophecies will often be interpretations of pictures or inner visions they see.[3]

Typically, prophets and seers teach others to receive revelation in the way that they receive it. For the prophet, this would be hearing the inward voice of the Holy Spirit. For the seer who receives revelation in a more visual way, this would be taught as dreams, mental pictures, visions that appear before their eyes (sometimes called an open vision), angelic messengers, and experiences in Heaven or in the unseen realm.

There are many different ways that God talks to seers, so each seer is different. Some seers are almost strictly spoken to through dreams, whereas some have the ability to use their spiritual eyes and see into the unseen realm as Elisha did:

And Elisha prayed, "O Lord, open his eyes so he may see." Then the Lord opened the servant's eyes, and he looked and saw the hills full of horses and chariots of fire all around Elisha (2 Kings 6:17).

ENDNOTES

1. Dennis Cramer, *School of Prophecy, Level One* (Williamsport, PA: Dennis Cramer Ministries, 1998), 54.

2. Paula A. Price, *The Prophet's Dictionary* (Tulsa, OK: Flaming Vision Publications, 2002), 494.

3. Cindy Jacobs, *The Voice of God* (Ventura, CA: Regal Books, 1995), 223.

CHAPTER 6

The Unseen Realm

"So we fix our eyes not on what is seen, but on what is unseen, for what is seen is temporary, but what is unseen is eternal" (2 Corinthians 4:18).

We have in this passage four different words that are important to understand: *seen, unseen, temporary,* and *eternal.* The *seen* is what we call the physical realm, that which is visible to the physical eye. This realm can be studied and experienced through our natural five senses of taste, touch, sound, sight, and smell.

The *unseen* is another realm. Like the physical realm, it also can be experienced with the five senses. The five senses of our physical body do not interact with the unseen realm, but we have five senses in our spirit that interact with this realm. The physical realm and spiritual realm are what Paul was writing about when he refers to the seen and unseen.

Then we have the *eternal* and the *temporary.* The eternal is any realm other than the physical. For example, ten billion years ago, God existed in the heavens and in the spirit. Ten billion years from now God will still exist in the heavens and in the spirit. When Paul writes of the temporary, he is speaking of this physical realm that began in Genesis 1 and continues only until it is replaced with the New Earth in Revelation 22. If you were to draw a line to represent time and it extended infinitely into the past and infinitely into the future, and if you were to put a one inch mark on this line, this would give you an idea of what the time-span of the physical realm looks like from Heaven's perspective. This is a good perspective to have when considering the reality of the spirit realm.

Many have stated that the spirit realm is just as real as the physical realm; this is in fact a huge understatement. The truth is that the spirit realm is far more real than the physical realm. In fact, if you were to die this very second while reading this book, you would immediately be dwelling in the spirit realm. You are one heartbeat away from existing entirely in the spirit realm. Yet some live their entire lives denying the existence of the spirit realm.

The spirit realm is far more real than the physical realm.

When an angel appears in the physical realm, people generally think that the angel came from Heaven. It is true that the Lord's angels do have their home in Heaven with God, but they can also surround us on the earth in the unseen realm, such as with Elisha and his servant in Second Kings 6. They sometimes manifest in the seen realm to speak a message, and then step back into the unseen realm, such as with Balaam in Numbers 22. At times this delivery of a message can take much time and warfare that we may not be fully aware of. For example, the angels Michael and Gabriel had to war together against the prince of Persia (possibly a regional evil spirit) to be able to finally break through 21 days of warfare and deliver a message to Daniel (see Dan. 10:13).

DEFINING THE TERMS

Some teachers in the Body of Christ have coined new extra-biblical terms for explaining three different realms. [Authors note: "extra-biblical" simply refers to things not in the Bible. This is not the same as anti-or unbiblical] Based on Paul using the phrase "third heaven" in Second Corinthians 12:2-4, they have extrapolated that if there is a third heaven, then it would stand to reason that there must be a first and second heaven, neither of which is mentioned by name in the Bible. Theologically, this is not a wrong assumption. However, when we begin to create new extra-biblical terms, we usually scare and divide from other parts of the Body of Christ. I have chosen to use biblical language as much as possible that I may be able to bring other more timid parts of the Church into new experience with the Holy Spirit.

When people refer to the first heaven they mean what the Bible calls the *seen realm*. When the second heaven is spoken of, it is what the Bible calls the *unseen realm,* which surrounds the physical realm. The term *third heaven* is only mentioned one time in Scripture and it is referred to as an experience that had happened once in 14 years and the author could not even describe this precious experience.

I know a man in Christ who fourteen years ago was caught up to the third heaven. Whether it was in the body or out of the body I do not know—God knows. And I know that this man—whether in the body or apart from the body I do not know, but God knows—was caught up to paradise. He heard inexpressible things, things that man is not permitted to tell (2 Corinthians 12:2-4).

Because the third heaven is only mentioned once and without description, I chose not to use this term casually. Consider that the third heaven must be something profound—in that it was indescribable and unusual—in that it happened once in 14 years. While we do have access to the heavenly realm and experiences, according to Paul the third heaven is altogether something different.

EXAMPLES OF THE UNSEEN REALM
ELISHA AND HIS SERVANT

"Go, find out where he is," the king ordered, "so I can send men and capture him." The report came back: "He is in Dothan." Then he sent horses and chariots and a strong force there. They went by night and surrounded the city. When the servant of the man of God got up and went out early the next morning, an army with horses and chariots had surrounded the city. "Oh, my lord, what shall we do?" the servant asked. "Don't be afraid," the prophet answered. "Those who are with us are more than those who are with them." And Elisha prayed, "O Lord, open his eyes so he may see." Then the Lord opened the servant's eyes, and he looked and saw the hills full of horses and chariots of fire all around Elisha (2 Kings 6:13-17).

In this story Elisha had been surrounded by enemy forces during the night. When the servant awoke and realized that they were surrounded, he was full of fear. Elisha, however, was calm, cool, and collected. He directed his servant not to be afraid and informed him that there were more forces on their side than the enemy had on his side.

Elisha was seeing into the unseen realm of the spirit. He prayed that his servant would be able to see as well. The servant received this impartation and was able to see what Elisha saw. My friend Harold Eberle has an interesting insight about how we see things in the spirit and how God communicates with us:

The servant received this impartation and was able to see what Elisha saw.

To see how spiritual dynamics relate to natural consequences, consider how the prophet Elisha and his servant became surrounded by enemy soldiers. When Elisha prayed for his servant's eyes to be opened to the spiritual world, "he saw; and behold, the mountain was full of horses and chariots of fire all around Elisha" (2 Kings 6:17 NKJV). Knowing that God was with him, Elisha had no fear. He prayed that God would strike the enemies with blindness, and they immediately went blind for a season.

This story is enlightening concerning how the spiritual realm appears to the one who can see into that realm. God communicates through visions. He uses pictures we can relate to in order to communicate what is going on in the spiritual world.

Concerning Elisha and his servant's vision, it is difficult to say whether horses and chariots actually existed in the spiritual world or if the horses and chariots that they saw represented the power of God that was available to defend them. For us today, horses and chariots would not be a very effective representation of God's power because one modern military machine such as a tank could defeat thousands of horses and chariots. Perhaps, then, if God wanted to reveal His power to us, He would show armies with all of the latest, most deadly equipment.

That reveals how realities in the spiritual realm are communicated to us in the natural realm. It is similar to the pictures one sees in dreams. There are true messages behind spiritual images, but the images are merely a form of communication.[1]

DANIEL SEES IN THE SPIRIT REALM

Daniel lived a life full of incredible spiritual experiences. In Daniel 10, Daniel sees into the unseen realm, but the men who were with him did not share in his experience. He had recently had a vision about a coming war and was emotionally disturbed by it for several weeks. One day, as Daniel was standing on the bank of the river Tigris, he began to see into the spirit realm:

> *On the twenty-fourth day of the first month, as I was standing on the bank of the great river, the Tigris, I looked up and there before me was a man dressed in linen, with a belt of the finest gold around his waist. His body was like chrysolite, his face like lightning, his eyes like flaming torches, his arms and legs like the gleam of burnished bronze, and his voice like the sound of a multitude. I, Daniel, was the only one who saw the vision; the men with me did not see it, but such terror overwhelmed them that they fled and hid themselves* (Daniel 10:4-7).

Daniel saw, and although the men didn't, they did sense a very strong presence, so strong that they actually fled and hid. How incredible that they were standing next to Daniel one minute and suddenly had the overwhelming urge to run away and hide! The vision continues with Daniel all by himself:

> *So I was left alone, gazing at this great vision; I had no strength left, my face turned deathly pale and I was helpless. Then I heard him speaking, and as I listened to him, I fell into a deep sleep, my face to the ground. A hand touched me and set me trembling on my hands and knees. He said, "Daniel, you who are highly esteemed, consider carefully the words I am about to speak to you, and stand up, for I have now been sent to you." And when he said this to me, I stood up trembling* (Daniel 10:8-11).

Daniel managed to stay for the vision, but he was physically overwhelmed.

Daniel managed to stay for the vision, but he was physically overwhelmed. From the outside, this must have been interesting to watch. Here is Daniel with a group of guys, when suddenly they bolt, looking terrified. Daniel is the only one left, and he turns pale and drops to the ground. Then trembling, he rises to his feet, yet in the physical, nothing is visible to make sense of this.

The Apostle John

The apostle John was under religious persecution and had been exiled to the island of Patmos. He wrote that on the Lord's Day, he was in the spirit (for perspective on what "in the spirit" means, see Chapter 14, "Worship in Spirit and in Truth"). Suddenly, he entered into a prophetic experience where he saw into the unseen realm.

I turned around to see the voice that was speaking to me. And when I turned I saw seven golden lampstands, and among the lampstands was someone "like a son of man," dressed in a robe reaching down to His feet and with a golden sash around His chest. His head and hair were white like wool, as white as snow, and His eyes were like blazing fire. His feet were like bronze glowing in a furnace, and His voice was like the sound of rushing waters. In His right hand He held seven stars, and out of His mouth came a sharp double-edged sword. His face was like the sun shining in all its brilliance.

When I saw Him, I fell at His feet as though dead. Then He placed His right hand on me and said: "Do not be afraid. I am the First and the Last. I am the Living One; I was dead, and behold I am alive forever and ever! And I hold the keys of death and Hades" (Revelation 1:9-18).

When it says that John "fell down as though dead," his physical body actually fell down in the physical realm. As he stood in the physical realm and watched a vision before him in the spirit realm, he was affected physically. In Revelation 1-3, John is in his physical body watching a vision with his spiritual eyes. It is not until the beginning of chapter 4 that John leaves his body behind. In Revelation 4, God calls John up and out of the earth: "Come up here" (Rev. 4:1), and the experience becomes an out-of-body experience.

Balaam and His Donkey

This is one of the most mysterious stories in the Book of Numbers. Balaam the prophet was rebelling against the word of the Lord. He had set out on his donkey and had two of his servants traveling along with him. The Word tells us that Balaam's donkey saw into the spirit realm and saw the angel of the Lord standing in the road with a drawn sword. The donkey turned away to save itself, but Balaam, who was dull to seeing because of his disobedience, became angry with the donkey. He began to beat the donkey to go down the road. Again, the donkey saw the angel and tried to get away by pressing up against a wall, thus crushing Balaam's foot. Balaam beat the donkey again. A third time the donkey saw the angel, and this time it just sat down under Balaam. This angered him again, and again he beat the donkey.

> *Balaam got up in the morning, saddled his donkey and went with the princes of Moab. But God was very angry when he went, and the angel of the Lord stood in the road to oppose him. Balaam was riding on his donkey and his two servants were with him. When **the donkey saw the angel of the Lord** standing in the road with a drawn sword in his hand, she turned off the road into a field. Balaam beat her to get her back on the road. Then the angel of the Lord stood in a narrow path between two vineyards, with walls on both sides. When **the donkey saw the angel of the Lord,** she pressed close to the wall, crushing Balaam's foot against it. So he beat her again. Then the angel of the Lord moved on ahead and stood in a narrow place where there was no room to turn, either to the right or to the left. When **the donkey saw the angel of the Lord,** she lay down under Balaam, and he was angry and beat her with his staff* (Numbers 22:21-27).

This story gets really weird when God gives the donkey the momentary ability to speak. The donkey asks why Balaam is beating her, and Balaam responds that the donkey is making a fool of him. He foolishly says that if he had a sword, he would kill his talking donkey. The donkey reasons with him that she has never acted in this way, and Balaam concedes that this is true. Then suddenly the Lord opens Balaam's eyes to the spirit realm. There standing in the unseen realm is the angel that was sent to kill him. The angel says that if the donkey hadn't turned away, he would have killed Balaam and would have left the donkey alive.

> *Then the Lord opened the donkey's mouth, and she said to Balaam, "What have I done to you to make you beat me these three times?" Balaam answered the donkey, "You have made a fool of me! If I had a sword in my hand, I would kill you right now." The donkey said to Balaam, "Am I not your own donkey, which you have always ridden, to this day? Have I been in the habit of doing this to you?" "No," he said. **Then the Lord opened Balaam's eyes,** and he saw the angel of the Lord standing in the road with his sword drawn. So he bowed low and fell facedown. The angel of the Lord asked him, "Why have you beaten your donkey these three times? I have come here to oppose you because your path is a reckless one before me.*

The donkey saw me and turned away from me these three times. If she had not turned away, I would certainly have killed you by now, but I would have spared her" (Numbers 22:28-33).

This opens up a discussion about animals and the spirit realm. Pastor Roland Buck, author of the classic book *Angels on Assignment,* shares about his dog having an awareness of the spirit realm:

Queenie, that's my dog... a purebred Great Dane... quietly "woofed" as she pressed her wet nose against my face. The time was 2:00 A.M. I knew what was up by now. That is the way she rouses me when she becomes aware that angelic visitors are in the house.[2]

Perhaps Balaam's donkey had a heightened awareness of spiritual beings because of the proximity of the anointing over time, or perhaps it is part of the nature of animals to be aware of the spirit realm.

From this sampling of Scripture we see that many Bible characters experienced and interacted with the unseen realm. As New Testament believers, we also have access and should experience this realm in our lives.

The unseen realm is neither good nor evil.

FINAL THOUGHTS

There are a lot of opinions about whether the spirit realm is good or bad, but as we look at Scripture we find that both angels and demons operate on this plane of existence. Even Jesus appears to Daniel and John in this realm. The unseen realm is neither good nor evil, in the same way that the physical realm is neither good nor evil. It is merely a plane of existence. Just as in the physical realm, the beings that dwell there can be good or evil. To say that everything in the unseen realm [or second heaven] is demonic is not biblical and we will be cutting ourselves off from a legitimate way that God speaks to us. Since we do not live in awareness of the spirit realm on a constant basis, we must use discernment when interacting with this realm.

ACTIVATION I

Put this prayer in your own words:

Lord,

I want communication from Heaven in my life. I ask that You would open the unseen realm to me. Lord, please remove all fear from my heart—fear of the unseen and fear of spiritual encounters. Lord, I want to receive all of the spiritual blessings that You have provided for me. I make myself available to Your many forms of communication.

ACTIVATION II

This exercise may take some more time.

First, ask the Lord to bring to your mind a friend or family member.

Second, ask the Lord to show you something about or around that person in the spirit realm. This could be an angel standing by them, Jesus, a demonic presence, a fruit of the Holy Spirit, objects such as weapons or chains, a special outfit such as armor or tribal clothing, etc.

Third, ask the Lord to give you insight into what you are seeing and how this translates into a word of encouragement for this individual.

Fourth, write down what you saw and what it means as if you were writing a letter to this person.

We will come back to this letter at the end of Chapter 8, "Discerning of Spirits."

ENDNOTES

1. Harold Eberle, *Victorious Eschatology* (Yakima, WA, Worldcast Pub., 2006), 156-157.

2. Charles and Frances Hunter, with Roland Buck, *Angels on Assignment* (Houston, TX: Hunter Books, 1979).

CHAPTER 7

Questions About the Angelic Realm

There have been literally hundreds of books written about angels. I have read dozens of them. My goal in writing this book has been to provide fresh perspective on age-old truths. Rather than addressing basic questions that can be answered by reading almost any book on the topic, (e.g., What do angels look like? How many angels are there? Are there bad angels?), I will focus in this chapter on some of the more difficult, unusual, and even controversial questions about the angelic.

Q: Do You See Angels All the Time?

A: As with all gifts of the Holy Spirit, we must step out in faith to activate the gift. For example, while the Holy Spirit will sometimes move sovereignly to heal someone, most of the time we must engage our faith. Jesus often commanded an act of obedience in order to activate faith for healing. For example, He said, "Go and show yourself to the priest," "Go wash the mud from your eyes," or "Pick up your bed and walk." In each case, physical healing occurred after the person responded in faith by obeying the command.

When the Holy Spirit gives a prophetic word, we must take part by cooperating with the Spirit and delivering the word. When you act in faith, you are stepping over into the things of the Kingdom realm—healing, prophecy, miracles, discerning of spirits, and so on. I don't see in the spirit realm all the time, but I can activate my faith, and I know that the Holy Spirit will meet my faith, and the gift of discerning of spirits will operate through me.

Q: Do You See Angels Like You See Other People?

A: When I am seeing angels, I see them in a manner similar to Elisha, Balaam, or Balaam's donkey. I see them superimposed over the natural realm. I do not see them as clearly as a person in the flesh, but my spirit eyes see them.

As we studied in the chapter on the spirit realm, there is scriptural precedent for one individual seeing an angelic being while the others standing by do not.

Q: Does Seeing in the Spirit Realm Mean That One Sees the Demonic as Well?

A: Yes, once your eyes are open, and you are able to see, you should be able to discern the spiritual roots of diseases, perhaps things in a person's past, or even at times the presence of demonic spirits. This is a good thing, because as we walk in the authority of Christ and the demonic shows up in our path, we can deal with it and push the Kingdom of God forward.

I have talked with many people who started seeing the dark side before they began to see the angels and the light side. I don't have an explanation for this, but I have a few speculative theories.

First, entertainment in our culture is full of horror and violence. This has polluted the spirit eyes of many and needs to be repented of so that cleansing can be released.

Second, a familiar spirit might be hanging around a family or individual because of a generational curse. This can be broken off by the blood of Jesus.

Third, satan is fully resisting the gift of discerning of spirits. If he can scare a person away from using his or her gift, then he has succeeded. As you continue to mature and press forward in your gifting, the other realms of discernment will begin to open up as well.

Q: Are There Female Angels?

A: There is no reference to an angel being a female in Scripture. This is an important point because the New Age movement has brought so much confusion into the Church in the Western World. Angels are most commonly portrayed as females—closely followed by a fat baby cherub with a bow and arrow—both of which are unscriptural.

There are female spiritual beings in Scripture, such as those mentioned in Zechariah 5:5-11. These verses are commonly used to teach that there are female angels. But if we study this passage closely, these beings are never referred to as angels.

Then the angel who was speaking to me came forward and said to me, "Look up and see what this is that is appearing." I asked, "What is it?" He replied, "It is a measuring basket." And he added, "This is the iniquity of the people throughout the land." Then the cover of lead was raised, and there in the basket sat a woman! He said, "This is wickedness," and he pushed her back into the basket and pushed the lead cover down over its mouth. Then I looked up—and there before me were two women, with wind in their wings! They had wings like those of a stork, and they lifted up the basket between heaven and earth. "Where are they taking the basket?" I asked the angel who was speaking to me. He replied, "To the country of Babylonia to build a house for it. When it is ready, the basket will be set there in its place" (Zechariah 5:5-11).

The angel standing next to Zechariah in his vision is referred to as masculine. Then he sees two women with wings like those of a stork appear and fly away.

The first wrong assumption is that angels commonly have wings; therefore, these must be angels. In the Bible, seraphim (see Isa. 6:2) and cherubim (see Ezek. 10:8) are clearly described as having wings, but they are a different class of spiritual beings, not angels. Angels are a specific class and order of being—not to be confused with other spiritual beings such as cherubim, seraphim, the four living creatures (see Rev. 4:8), and the seven spirits of God (see Isa. 11; Rev. 4:5). If you look over the many references to angels in the Bible, you will find that the majority of them appear looking like men (not with wings). Hebrews 13:2 says, *"Do not forget to entertain strangers, for by so doing some people have entertained angels without knowing it."* If all angels had big Hollywood wings, then this verse would not make sense.

An interesting detail is that Zechariah says that the wings were like those of a stork. Nowhere else in the Bible does it say that angels have wings like a stork. If Zechariah were trying to say that these two women were angels, he could have said that they had wings like an angel. Instead he chose to describe them as something completely unique to his vision. As an additional note, God had told the Israelites that the stork was an unclean and detestable animal, so this vision was a negative picture (see Lev. 11:19).

Could it be that Zechariah was confused—perhaps he had never seen an angel, or he couldn't tell that they were female angels? This is an invalid assertion because he is standing next to an angel during the encounter. When looking at the whole of his book, Zechariah is not ignorant of the angelic realm. Zechariah could have said that two female angels came in a vision, but instead he described what he actually saw in this interesting vision—that is, two women with wings like those of a stork.

There is no direct reference to an angel being represented in feminine form in the Bible, but there are many references to feminine spirit beings. Examples include the two women in Zechariah 5, the woman and the dragon in Revelation 12, the whore of Babylon in Revelation 17, and the spirit of wisdom, which is referred to in the feminine throughout the Book of Proverbs (see Prov. 1:20-33; 4:5-9; 8; 9).

Q: Do Angels Have Gender?

A: Let's look at a passage that is commonly used to say that angels are without gender:

That same day the Sadducees, who say there is no resurrection, came to Him with a question. *"Teacher," they said, "Moses told us that if a man dies without having children, his brother must marry the widow and have children for him. Now there were seven brothers among us. The first one married and died, and since he had no children, he left his wife to his brother. The same thing happened to the second and third brother, right on down to the seventh. Finally, the woman died. Now then, at the resurrection, whose wife will she be of the seven, since all of them were married to her?"*

*Jesus replied, "You are in error because you do not know the Scriptures or the power of God. **At the resurrection people will neither marry nor be given in marriage; they will be like the angels in heaven.** But about the resurrection of the dead—have you not read what God said to you, 'I am the God of Abraham, the God of Isaac, and the God of Jacob'? He is not the God of the dead but of the living." When the crowds heard this, they were astonished at His teaching* (Matthew 22:30-33).

Many have stretched this verse to mean that angels are without gender because they neither marry nor are given in marriage. What is this verse really saying? When Jesus says that people will be like the angels in heaven at the resurrection, how does this have anything to do with gender? If we are to believe that angels are genderless and we are going to be like them, then once we are resurrected will we also be genderless? Obviously not!

Consider that every single reference out of the hundreds in Scripture always refer to angels as masculine. To conclude that angels are genderless and that is why they don't marry is like saying that people with the gift of celibacy (see 1 Cor. 7:7) are genderless and that is why they don't get married. Some have gone so far as to assume that since angels do not reproduce, they must be without gender. The truth is, angels are not a race, they are individual creations and that is why they do not reproduce.

Angels are not a race, they are individual creations.

Suppose we were to stretch the meaning the other way and say that since every reference in Scripture shows that all angels are masculine, if we are to be like them, then all women will turn into men at the resurrection. Surely no one would argue this as a valid point.

When Jesus says that we will be like the angels, the statement may have more obvious implications, such as having eternal life, glorified bodies, and sinless living. Perhaps Jesus was actually answering their question, which had nothing to do with the gender of angels. He might have been saying that we will live in the heavenly realm like the angels and not have the difficulties and complications of this earthly life, such as death, marriage, and remarriage.

Q: What Is a Typical Physical Response to an Angelic Encounter?

A: I believe that everyone reacts differently. I would like to quote from one of my favorite books on angels, *Angels, Elect and Evil* by Fred Dickason:

When angels do appear, their presence produces various effects upon men. No special effect is noted upon Joseph except the allaying of his human concern about Mary and his obedience to the revealed will of God (see Matt. 1:18-25).

Mental and emotional agitation came upon Mary when Gabriel announced to her the news of the virgin birth of Christ. Nevertheless, she conversed with him and accepted his message as from God (see Luke 1:29, 34, 38). Zacharias was troubled and gripped by fear when an angel appeared to him in the temple (see Luke 1:12). The shepherds to whom the angelic messenger announced the birth of Christ were very much afraid (see Luke 2:9) at first, yet they rationally investigated the news and marveled at the message (see Luke 2:15-18).

Mental and physical weakness, sometimes accompanied by complete lack of composure, results from angels' presence. Consider the Roman guards who saw the angel who rolled back the stone from Christ's tomb. They trembled from fear and became as dead (see Matt. 28:4). When Daniel saw an unusual manlike creature of brilliant appearance, he was left without strength and comeliness (see Dan. 10:8). Even those who did not see the vision trembled greatly. Strange sensations caused them to flee from Daniel's presence with fear. Animals may in the will of God see angels and so hesitate or fall, as did Balaam's donkey (see Num. 22:26-28, 31).[1]

Q: Why Didn't Jesus Die for the Sins of Fallen Angels?

A: Many theologians have suggested that the main difference between humans and angels is that angels are not a race of beings. Humans are a race of beings; we reproduce, we die, and we have a bloodstream in our body. When Jesus came and died for us, Philippians 2 tells us that Jesus became a part of the human race. Romans 5 speaks of how Jesus established a new bloodstream. On the earth now, there are two races, those who are in the bloodline of Adam, the fallen first man, and those who are in the bloodline of the last Adam, Jesus Christ (see 1 Cor. 15:44-49). That is why we are new creatures and why Second Peter 1:4 speaks of us being partakers of the divine nature. As a race, Jesus could die once for all (see Heb. 10:10) and establish a new race.

Angels, however, are each an individual creation. They are not a blood line (they may not even have blood), and they don't reproduce. If Jesus were to die for their sins, He would have to die for each fallen angel individually, over and over again, perhaps millions of times to be able to die and resurrect for each one.

Q: Is It Imbalanced to Focus So Much on Angels?

A: I have been writing this book for many years, and I have felt odd at times writing so much about the spirit realm and angels. In fact, there has even been an outcry in certain church circles against the prophetic movement and its focused teaching on the angelic realm. I have sought the Lord about if we are in imbalance by talking about and giving focus to angels. The response I received from the Lord was surprising.

In essence, the Lord showed me that the root issue of those who have a problem with talking about angels and the spirit realm is that they do not accurately understand what a Christian is. The Lord took me to Hebrews 1.

So He became as much superior to the angels as the name He has inherited is superior to theirs. For to which of the angels did God ever say, "You are My Son; today I have become Your Father?" Or again, "I will be His Father, and He will be My Son?"

And again, when God brings His firstborn into the world, He says, "Let all God's angels worship Him." In speaking of the angels He says, "He makes His angels winds, His servants flames of fire." But about the Son He says, "Your throne, O God, will last for ever and ever, and righteousness will be the scepter of Your kingdom. You have loved righteousness and hated wickedness; therefore God, Your God, has set You above Your companions by anointing You with the oil of joy."...To which of the angels did God ever say, "Sit at My right hand until I make Your enemies a footstool for Your feet"? Are not all angels ministering spirits sent to serve those who will inherit salvation? (Hebrews 1:4-14).

The Church understands that Jesus is greater and higher than the angels, but there has been confusion as to whether we are higher than the angels or vice versa. The answer is simple: If you are in Christ, then you are higher than the angels. We are to be *"hid with Christ in God"* (see Col. 3:3), and if we abide in Him, then He will abide in us (see John 15:4). Christ is higher than the angels, and we are in Him; thus, we are in a higher place than the angels.

Several other passages shed light on the concept that angels are lower than believers. The apostle Paul tells us that we are going to judge angels, *Do you not know that we will judge angels? How much more the things of this life!"* (1 Cor. 6:3). The Book of Hebrews tells us that angels have been sent forth to serve believers, *"Are not all angels ministering spirits sent to serve those who will inherit salvation?"* (Heb 1:14). This being the case, consider the words of Jesus: *"No servant is greater than his master"* (John 15:20). Clearly, this is just a sampling of many verses that show that in the Kingdom of Heaven, angels are not in a higher position than a believer. If we are put off by trying to understand beings like angels who occupy a lower place, then we clearly have not grasped the Kingdom that we are a part of.

Christians need to stop being so impressed by those claiming to have seen an angel and realize that every time we look at a fellow believer, we are looking at a being with a divine nature (see 2 Pet. 1:4). A Christian is of much greater stature than any angel. When I am looking at a fellow believer, I am literally looking at the only type of being that has ever been given the very *mind of Christ* (1 Cor. 2:16). In fact, Scripture says that we have been given such a high level of insight into the Kingdom of Heaven that, *"...even angels long to look into these things"* (1 Peter 1:12). A believer simultaneously dwells in three worlds because they exist in the physical realm, the spiritual realm, and the heavenly realms with Christ (see Eph. 2:6).

Christians need to stop being so impressed by those claiming to have seen an angel

Consider this: In the beginning only God existed; then at some point, He created the angels. This was God's first act of creation. Then God created earth and its inhabitants: This was God's second act of creation. The third and most recent act of creation in all of eternity past was when through Christ's bloodline God created new creatures in Christ Jesus (see 2 Cor. 5:17). You, as a new creature in Christ, are literally the most recent creation God has made in all of history, and we are the only new thing on this old planet. We have been left on this planet as ambassadors, priests, kings, and oracles to mold and transform this planet until God comes back and performs His fourth and final act of creation, giving us a new Heaven and a new earth that is more suitable for such amazing new creatures to inhabit with Him eternally.

Until our perspective shifts to seeing ourselves and each other properly through God's eyes, we will still be overly impressed with those who have seen angels and operate in the spirit realm. The spirit realm needs to be demystified and understood by the average Christian, keeping in mind that the average Christian is much more amazing than we have been made to believe.

A FINAL WORD

In this chapter I have responded to eight very difficult and interesting questions regarding the angelic. I may have caused more questions to come to mind as you read this chapter. My goal was not to answer every question about angels; this book is not an in-depth study of angels. I just wanted to get you, the reader, curious and thinking more about this subject. It is fine if you disagree with my answers, I have tried to answer not from a personal preference or bias; my desire is to base my answers upon a biblical foundation. If you would like to know more of what the Bible teaches about angels, I would highly recommend above all the others, *Angels, Elect and Evil* by Fred Dickason.

ENDNOTES

1. C. Fred Dickason, *Angels, Elect and Evil* (Chicago, IL: Moody Press, 1975), 37.

—PART TWO—

SPIRITUAL
SIGHT

CHAPTER 8

Discerning of Spirits

Discerning of spirits is the most misunderstood of all the spiritual gifts. Because of the confusion surrounding this gift, clear biblical teaching on discerning of spirits is needed. The gift of discerning of spirits and the natural ability of discernment are not the same thing. There are many people who have a high level of sensitivity in the natural or emotional realm. This can even be taught through a heightened self-awareness to your emotional state, as explained by Daniel Goleman in his groundbreaking work, *Emotional Intelligence*.[1]

The difference between natural abilities and the nine spiritual gifts listed in First Corinthians 12 is that spiritual gifts are supernatural in nature. For example, a "word of knowledge" is something supernatural, not something that could be attained through natural means. The same is true of the supernatural gift of healing; it supersedes the laws of the natural world. This applies to all nine of the gifts, but our focus here is on the gift of discerning of spirits.

In our culture, we have accepted that someone can be very discerning, but this is a natural intuitive ability. The spiritual gift in First Corinthians 12 is something unique. There is a correlation between natural and supernatural discernment in that both gifts help to inform an individual what is in the atmosphere or environment surrounding them. Natural discernment informs what is in the natural, emotional, or interpersonal realm, whereas supernatural discernment informs what is in the spiritual realm.

Supernatural discernment typically divides that information into four different areas: (1) the working of the Holy Spirit, (2) the working of the demonic, (3) the working of the human spirit, and (4) the working of heavenly beings.

Another reason that the gift of discerning of spirits has been misunderstood is that the gift has been abused. Many believe that discerning of spirits is the ability to know another person's secret sin and have used it as justification for harboring attitudes of suspicion, criticism, and accusation. Good-hearted people don't want to operate in this distorted version of discerning of spirits.

Many believe that discerning of spirits is the ability to know another person's secret sin

---

I have heard major church leaders comment that if they had to choose to remove one of the nine gifts of the Spirit, they "would absolutely choose to remove the gift of discerning of spirits because no other gift has singlehandedly caused as much damage to the Body of Christ." That comment only makes sense in light of the misuse of this gift. Let's look closer at what the gift of discerning of spirits truly is.

THREE ROOT WORDS

In the Bible the words *judgment* and *discernment* can be used synonymously at times. There are actually three root words in the Greek for the word *judgment*.[2] This gives us a strong insight into the nature of discernment.

The first root word in the Greek is *anakrino*. In *Vine's Dictionary* the base meaning of this word is the ability to distinguish. We should always operate under this type of discernment.

> *The man without the Spirit does not accept the things that come from the Spirit of God, for they are foolishness to him, and he cannot understand them, because they are spiritually discerned* [anakrino] (1 Corinthians 2:14).

The second root word in Greek is *dokimazo*, the base meaning of which is to test or prove.

> *Hypocrites! You can discern* [dokimazo] *the face of the sky and of the earth, but how is it you do not discern* [dokimazo] *this time?* (Luke 12:56 NKJV).

This use of discernment is sometimes appropriate as a Christian. For example we are told to test the spirits (see 1 John 4:1) or judge our prophecies (see 1 Thess. 5:21).

The third root word for judgment in Greek is *krino*, which actually means to condemn. This is never the role of a Christian! We should distinguish good from evil, and we should even test and prove at times, but condemnation is off-limits for the believer.

Do not judge [krino], *or you too will be judged* [krino]. *For in the same way you judge* [krino] *others, you will be judged* [krino], *and with the measure you use, it will be measured to you* (Matthew 7:1-2).

From these three root words for judgment, we learn that there are two types of judgment which are good and one that is not. As we move in discernment we need to remember that Jesus said that we are to judge with *righteous* judgment.

Do not judge according to appearance, but judge with righteous judgment (John 7:24 NKJV).

THE FOUR CATEGORIES

Because of a lack of biblical teaching, the gift of discerning of spirits has been misunderstood in the church to be criticism, suspicion, and condemnation. The truth is that it is a supernatural gift from the Holy Spirit to be operated through love. There are four types of spirits you can discern: The Holy Spirit, heavenly spirits, the human spirit, and demonic spirits. Discerning of spirits helps us know which of these four spirits we are interacting with.

1. The Holy Spirit

During the mass confusion on the day of Pentecost (Acts 2), Peter, having discerning of spirits in operation, stood in front of the crowd and declared that what was happening was a move of the Holy Spirit. In Acts 8, the church sent Peter and John to go check out Philip's conversion of Samaritans. It required discernment on the part of Peter to acknowledge that what was happening with Philip was the work of the Holy Spirit. It took obedience and discernment to bring salvation and baptism in the Holy Spirit to the house of Cornelius. When God is showing you something that is outside your comfort zone, it usually requires the operation of discerning of spirits to accept new truth.

John the Baptist also discerned the presence of the Holy Spirit before baptizing Jesus:

Then John gave this testimony: "I saw the Spirit come down from heaven as a dove and remain on Him. I would not have known Him, except that the One who sent me to baptize with water told me, 'The man on whom you see the Spirit come down and remain is He who will baptize with the Holy Spirit.' I have seen and I testify that this is the Son of God" (John 1:32-34).

Another example of discerning the Holy Spirit comes from my wife, Karen Welton:

One night, a group of seven or eight of my friends and I got together at one of our homes. We originally intended to play board games, but I felt like doing something different. I had a lingering desire to invite the presence of God into the room, so I suggested we put on some worship music instead. I could feel the atmosphere was pregnant with a potential visitation. My friend put on some worship music, and the presence of the Lord filled his living room. We found ourselves face down on the floor worshipping Jesus.

I could feel the atmosphere was pregnant with a potential visitation.

In the spirit, I saw water filling up the room. It started as only a couple inches deep as we all lay on the floor, but the water grew deeper as we worshipped. I was aware of the presence of angels in the room, seven in total. In the center of the room, I sensed something different. I thought, "there must be a large angel standing there because I sense something powerful swirling around in the middle." I tried to discern what kind of angel could be this powerful, and why was it different from all the others? I realized it wasn't an angel at all, it was a vortex of water about 4 or 5 feet wide swirling around powerfully and overflowing from the top and filling the room. I was seeing the manifest presence of the Holy Spirit.

By now the water had reached shoulder level, and I moved to the center of the vortex and laid face down. Within ten minutes, without me saying anything, three others moved and laid down in the center of the room with me. The water grew deeper as the power source overflowed, filling the room with more water. God was literally pouring out His Spirit on us!

At this point the water was higher than our heads. I saw one of my friends stand up in the middle of the room and place a flattened hand at the top of where I saw the water level in the spirit, just over his head. I looked at him incredulously and said, "That's exactly where the water level is! You see the vortex of water, too?" No one had said anything this whole time, and I didn't know if anyone else had seen the water filling the room in the spirit realm.

My friend said, "There is a pillar of water right here, and it's this high; on top of the pillar of water, it turns into a pillar of fire coming down from the ceiling. If you put your hand right here, you can feel a change in pressure." He held his hand flat in the air, bouncing it a little with the water. I knew about the large pillar of water, but had not realized there was a pillar of fire on top.

Many of us put our hands at the same level, and we all felt a slight change in pressure where the pillar of water turned into a pillar of fire.

My friend, Ben Valence shares one of his experiences of discerning the presence of the Holy Spirit:

It was like any other week at youth group, when, during worship, the Lord asked me to do something. As I pressed in, the Lord told me I was holding a bucket and to go around and pour something over everyone. Feeling kind of silly, I went over to Jon and told him what the Lord had told me, and he just said to do it. I went around the whole church pouring something over people, thinking that I must look crazy.

When I got back to Jon, I asked what he was seeing. I was amazed when he told me that there were two big angels on stage and that there was water running over the stage down onto the whole sanctuary. The water was mixed with oil, and being only ankle deep even the people lying on the ground praising the Lord were not fully submersed in it. I was going around with the bucket actually scooping up this water and oil and washing it over everyone there. Even though I looked silly in the physical, I was doing something in the spirit realm that was much more profound. All that the Lord told me was that I had a bucket, but I believed and obeyed, and after hearing what was going on the spirit realm, I am so glad I followed.

2. Heavenly Spirits

The Bible is full of references to angels and other heavenly creatures. Some of the clearest examples of discernment functioning would include Elisha seeing the heavenly host while his servant did not (see 2 Kings 6), or Balaam's donkey seeing the angel in the road three times before Balaam's eyes were opened (see Num. 22). When this operation of discernment is taking place, one individual may be aware of the presence of the heavenly spirit, while others around are not aware. This happened several times in the Word, such as when Jesus was being spoken to by the Father and those around only heard thunder (see John 12:28-29). Another example is when Jesus knocked Paul off his donkey, and the soldiers with Paul couldn't tell what was happening (see Acts 9:7).

One day in autumn I was driving home from work when I saw a large angel dressed in purple appear very abruptly in the road ahead of me. He had a large sword, which he gripped with both hands and pointed at me. I heard him say to me in my spirit, "Slow down now!" This was not a request, but rather a command. As soon as I saw him in purple I thought to myself, "Purple is a royal color, so this must be important." I slowed down immediately. As I arrived at the point where he had been standing, there was a sharp turn which I was familiar with. The only difference was that the car that had been ahead of me had completely stopped on the other side of the blind corner. If I had not slowed down, I would have plowed into his car at 40-50 miles per hour, most certainly killing the passengers of the other car and likely myself as well.

Equipping Angels

Another time, around the Christmas of 2002, I attended a conference with about 6000 youth in Niagara Falls, NY. During worship I began to see something I had never seen. In the center of the packed out civic center, I saw four large angels, easily one hundred or more feet tall. They each had a branding iron in their hand. At first I could not see what the brand said, but then they began to use the brand on specific individuals. They would place the branding iron across the chest of a person and left a label branded on them. I saw words like *Sanctified, Holy Unto the Lord, Nazarite,* and *Prophet to the Nations.* I could see this brand on different individuals for the remainder of the conference. Occasionally, I come across other individuals who were not at this specific meeting, but who also have a brand on their chests. I believe that this is occurring at many times and places as a commissioning—similar to Isaiah 6 and the angel consecrating Isaiah with coal from the fire.

Karen and I were attending a conference a couple of years ago in Columbus, Ohio. There were several well-known prophetic ministers there as speakers. As one of them finished his message and moved into ministry time, I saw something very unusual. The minister said that God was going to commission fivefold ministers that night. When he said this, a large angel appeared near the front of the sanctuary. This 15-20 foot tall angel had the word *equipping* written across his chest. He was standing very properly with cloths draped over his arm, which he held in front of him, reminiscent of a waiter at a fancy restaurant. The minister had the whole congregation line up and come to the front to have hands laid on them. As he did this, the "equipping" angel would lay one of his cloths over the shoulders of specific individuals. Once the cloth was laid on a person, I was able to read it. The cloths read *Apostle, Prophet, Evangelist, Pastor,* or *Teacher.* The Lord gave me understanding that these were mantles He was placing upon His leaders for the service of equipping the Church.

3. The Human Spirit

The Book of Acts contains many clear examples of this operation of discernment. For example, Peter confronts Simon the sorcerer about his evil heart motivations, Peter confronts Ananias and Sapphira about their lying, and Paul confronts the sorcerer Elymas for his evil heart. In other books, we find Paul confronting Peter about his hypocrisy, Jesus speaking of Nathanael's nature when first meeting him, and the many times that Jesus perceived the thoughts of others. These are all clear examples of discerning of spirits operating to discern the state of the human soul or spirit.

On one occasion, when I was praying for the sick, I saw something unique about the woman I was about to pray for. Before she told me what illness she was suffering with, I saw spears stuck in her from all directions in the spirit realm. They were about ten feet long and literally stuck out of her in every direction. I got the sense that she was okay when she didn't move, but that any person coming close to her would cause pain by unintentionally moving the spears in the unseen realm.

Before she told me what illness she was suffering with, I saw spears stuck in her from all directions in the spirit realm.

The woman told me she had anxiety, depression, chronic fatigue, fibromyalgia, Epstein Barr virus, and many other similar ailments. I described to her what I had seen in the spirit, and she said that what I saw perfectly described her. She literally did not want hands laid on her when I prayed for her because it would cause her pain.

Some of the spears had writing on them which explained what they were and how they had arrived there (such as hate, disappointment, and fear). We spent some time forgiving individuals who had hurt her, releasing word curses, and dealing with many heart issues. As we processed these issues, the spears were being removed in the spirit. By the time we finished that night, she was able to give me a big hug without pain. I later received an email from the group leader testifying that this individual has received a tremendous breakthrough in her health.

Consider how many times the church has read the following passage and yet we have missed a big clue into discernment. *"In addition to all this, take up the shield of faith, with which you can extinguish all the flaming arrows of the evil one."* (Eph. 6:16) The evil one is shooting spiritual, not literal arrows at believers. I often see believers riddled with arrows from the evil one, we need to discern in this realm so that we can bring healing to one another.

The Lord gave me an insight into why I see so many swords, spears, and other weapons stuck into people in the spirit. We see in Ephesians 6:17 that when words are in the hands of the Holy Spirit, those words are the sword of the Holy Spirit: *"... the sword of the Spirit, which is the word of God."*

Simply stated—*in the spirit, words equal swords*—so with our mouths we also wield swords. We can use our words with the Holy Spirit as a scalpel to bring healing and restoration into the lives of others, or we can use words in a destructive manner which spiritually stabs and injures others. *"Reckless words pierce like a sword, but the tongue of the wise brings healing."* (Prov. 12:18)

I commonly see objects stuck in individuals which represent emotional wounds and words that have been released against them. Often these are blocking an individual's ability to receive a physical healing they need. Forgiveness is often all that is needed. Other times the words that have been spoken against them need to be renounced, rejected, or condemned (see Isa. 54:17). This is one way that discerning of spirits can operate to bring emotional and physical healing.

Another example of discerning the human spirit comes from my friend Ben Valence.

I have had back problems for over five years. Every six months to a year, I would blow out my back, and the pain was so intense that I would have to take a month off from work. It hurt so bad I could barely make it out of bed even with help. In addition to the back problems, I was getting random fevers and other sicknesses. I finally went to the doctor, but he could not find a cause for the problems. It got to the point where I was getting fevers once a week and losing sleep. One night we were at Jon's house having a time of worship and prayer. Jon then led us in a time of activation, praying over each of us. As I was standing in the middle with my eyes closed, everyone else stood behind me saying, "It's right here; do you feel it?" As they were saying this I could feel something piercing my back and going through my chest to my stomach. I could feel it being poked in and out, and it hurt badly. I told them to stop and asked what they were doing because it hurt. They pointed out that they were seeing something in the air behind my back. When Jon put his hand in the air and pressed down on this invisible object, I could feel him touching something that I could not see with my physical eyes, but could definitely feel in the natural, piercing my flesh. After asking the Lord what caused this item, which seemed to be a pipe or sword, we stopped and prayed. Then Jon grabbed the sword (in the unseen realm) and slowly pulled it out of my back. As he pulled, I felt the blade slide through my chest and then through my back. After he removed the item from my back, he prayed over me again. As soon as the blade was gone I felt a relief wash over my body and a peace flood my senses. Waking up the next morning, I could not believe how good I felt. Since that night the fevers and all other sicknesses have left me, but best of all, I no longer have any problems with my back. God is so good. My back has been healed now since 2005.

I felt the blade slide through my chest and then through my back.

Is the human soul/spirit essentially good or bad?

There is a teaching in the Church that has caused a lot of confusion regarding how we view the human spirit/soul. This teaching says that the spirit of a believer is perfected, but the *soul* and *body* are defined as "the flesh," which is evil. Clearly stated, the flesh is fundamentally evil and the spirit is fundamentally perfect and holy. This teaching creates a never-ending interior struggle between the soul and the spirit. This inner struggle concept has become prevalent throughout much of the modern Church. Yet the Bible does not teach this and this is not an accurate definition of *the flesh*.

The idea that the spirit of a person is perfect while the person's soul/body comprise the evil flesh is a fundamentally flawed, erroneous teaching. The Bible does not even teach that we have perfected spirits or that our souls are evil. This concept has come from a misunderstanding of Hebrews 12:23:

> *But you have come to Mount Zion, to the city of the living God, the heavenly Jerusalem. You have come to thousands upon thousands of angels in joyful assembly, to the church of the firstborn, whose names are written in heaven. You have come to God, the Judge of all, to **the spirits of the righteous made perfect**, to Jesus the mediator of a new covenant, and to the sprinkled blood that speaks a better word than the blood of Abel* (Hebrews 12:22-24).

Notice that the context of **the spirits of righteous men made perfect** is in reference to those who are already in Heaven. It is not accurate to use this verse to claim that Jesus perfects the human spirit at salvation. These were the righteous men of Hebrews 11 who have died and gone on to Heaven before us.

Secondly, the Bible states that the spirit of a believer can still be defiled after salvation:

> *Therefore, having these promises, beloved, let us cleanse ourselves from all defilement of flesh and spirit, perfecting holiness in the fear of God* (2 Corinthians 7:1 NASB).

This contradicts the idea that the spirit of a believer is already perfected.

Regarding the soul, the Lord has never condemned the human soul as an evil thing. In fact, He made the human soul before the Fall of Man. Adam and Eve both had souls. If the human soul were inherently evil, it would not have existed in Eden. To equate the soul with the flesh is inaccurate. Consider that Jesus instructed us to love the Lord with all our heart, soul, mind and strength (see Mark 12:30). The word *spirit* isn't even on the list, and if the soul is equal to the flesh, how could we possibly love God with our evil flesh?

Since our flesh nature is not composed of the soul and the body, then what is the flesh? *The flesh* refers to a person's lower nature. This lower nature in Scripture is called *the carnal nature, the flesh, the old nature, the body of death,* and *the old man.* The flesh is the internal part of humankind that is inclined toward evil desires. The flesh operates in all three realms of the human design: the spirit, soul, and body; every human being has a portion that is inclined toward unhealthy appetites. This is *the flesh.*

"The flesh" refers to a person's lower nature.

As long as we continue to confuse the soul with the flesh, we will continue to see our own soul as if it were our enemy. A wrong interpretation of the following verse has caused much of the confusion regarding this topic. Let's look at it with new eyes:

> *For the word of God is living and powerful, and sharper than any two-edged sword, piercing even to the division of soul and spirit, and of joints and marrow, and is a discerner of the thoughts and intents of the heart* (Hebrews 4:12 NKJV).

When we read this verse believing that our spirit is good and our soul is bad, we create a division within ourselves that looks like this:

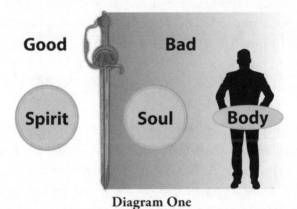

Diagram One

This diagram represents the belief of dualism, the division of soul from spirit. Yet look at this verse again. It actually says that the Word of God divides the soul and spirit; it is not saying that the Word divides the soul from the spirit as if one is good and one is bad. The Word divides both the soul and the spirit. Reading this verse correctly shows that the Word of God divides both the soul and spirit, you can see that an accurate division looks like this:

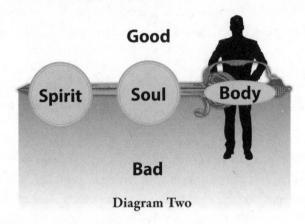

Diagram Two

The dividing sword pierces both the soul and the spirit. When you live according to the misinterpretation of diagram one, the spirit is placed in a lifelong battle against the soul. Also your discernment is slanted in thinking that the spirit is always good and the soul is always bad. The Bible does not support the teaching of a good spirit and an evil soul; this concept is actually a Gnostic heresy of the first century.

During the early Church, the Gnostics taught that the spirit was good and the physical/emotional realms were evil, and therefore Jesus could not have come to Earth in an actual physical body. They taught that Jesus came to Earth only as an ethereal spirit-being. This teaching is heretical because it negates the truth of Jesus shedding His human blood for the remission of sin. The Gnostics gained so many followers in the early Church that John wrote his first epistle in response to their heresy.

*That which was from the beginning, which we have heard, which we have **seen with our eyes, which we have looked at and our hands have touched**—this we proclaim concerning the Word of life. The life appeared; we have seen it and testify to it, and we proclaim to you the eternal life, which was with the Father and has appeared to us. We proclaim to you what we **have seen and heard**, so that you also may have fellowship with us. And our fellowship is with the Father and with His Son, Jesus Christ* (1 John 1:1-3).

John was writing to prove, as an eyewitness, that Jesus was not an ethereal ghost, but a real, physical person. John was the disciple who leaned his head upon Jesus' chest, and he knew that Jesus was not merely a spirit. He wrote saying that those who claim Jesus didn't have a physical body are actually anti-Christ.

> *Dear friends, do not believe every spirit, but test the spirits to see whether they are from God, because many false prophets have gone out into the world. This is how you can recognize the Spirit of God: Every spirit that **acknowledges that Jesus Christ has come in the flesh** is from God, but every spirit that does not acknowledge Jesus is not from God. This is the spirit of the antichrist, which you have heard is coming and even now is already in the world* (1 John 4:1-3).

The ancient Gnostics taught according to Diagram One. This teaching has been passed through the ages and many modern Christians are still taught that the soul and body comprise the flesh, but the Bible teaches nothing of the sort.

Actually the body is referred to as the temple of the Holy Spirit (see 1 Cor. 3:16; 6:19), and the apostle Paul said that exercising the physical body is of value (1 Tim. 4:8).

The soul is never used in the Bible as a negative term. Typically, those who are influenced by Gnostic teaching refer negatively to things as being *soulish, of the soul, of the soul realm,* or as being related to *soul ties, soul power,* etc. But biblically speaking, there is nothing inherently evil about the soul. We are not in a battle against our own soul.

There is a struggle against the flesh, but the flesh is not the same as the soul. To follow the Gnostic heresy to its reasonable application, we must: 1) become completely spirit, 2) we must suppress our soul, or 3) we must pit the spirit against the soul for the rest of our lives. Thankfully, none of these options reflects biblical truth.

In practical application, when we discern the human spirit/soul, we may discern the good things about someone, which reside in the part above the sword or the Lord may show us the negative things, which are below the sword in their "flesh." Discerning in the area of the human spirit/soul can aquire either good or bad information in the spirit realm.

4. Demonic Spirits

There are many examples of discerning of spirits in operation throughout the Gospels, especially if we look more closely at the healing miracles of Jesus. For example, consider this story again closely:

And behold, there was a woman who had a spirit of infirmity eighteen years, and was bent over and could in no way raise herself up. But when Jesus saw her, He called her to Him and said to her, "Woman, you are loosed from your infirmity." And He laid His hands on her, and immediately she was made straight, and glorified God (Luke 13:11-13 NKJV).

In the physical realm, the only thing that could be known was that the woman was bent over and that she had been in that condition for eighteen years. With the gift of discerning of spirits in operation, Jesus identified the root cause as a spirit of infirmity. So often the operation of discerning of spirits is overlooked, but it is in clear use all throughout the Word.

A Haunted Bathroom

For one of the weeks that I was in Brazil in 2002, our team was staying in a very nice four-star hotel. The only problem was that my bathroom was haunted. Seriously—the bedroom was fine; I slept fine; I had no nightmares—but when I was in the shower, something odd began to happen. The shower was a four wall glass shower stall. I had a general creepy feel about the bathroom from the beginning, but it was not until I turned on the water that things escalated. When I stepped into the shower and turned on the water, in the natural there was nothing out of the ordinary, but my spiritual sight saw the water as blood. Instead of seeing water splash off the glass walls, I was seeing blood splashing on the glass and running down. This was absolutely terrifying. I had the sense that someone had been stabbed to death in this shower stall. I told my roommate; we prayed over the bathroom all week, and by the end of the week, the feelings and sight had subsided considerably. This was one of my very first encounters like this, so although I did not have a full breakthrough victory, I did learn a lot that week. In the end I do not know whether someone had actually been killed there or if the spirit of fear was harassing us.

Another example of discernment and the demonic realm comes from my friend Benjamin Valence:

A group of us had gathered at Jon's house for a night of prayer and worship when the Lord tugged on my heart to come outside. Soon after stepping out the door, the Lord told me to take off my shoes and socks and go for a walk. I found it a little weird, but I followed his instructions. I was amazed to find myself feeling and sensing what was going on in the spirit at every house I passed. It is hard for me to explain what I mean; it was like I was feeling with my feet instead of my hands, and it was amazing. Even though it was cold outside, I could feel heat rushing through my toes and up my legs at houses where the Holy Spirit was moving. As I pressed on, the feelings got more intense until finally I came to a bridge. The bridge crossed over to the east side of town, and after passing over the bridge I could feel the atmosphere change for the worse. I not only felt the demonic, but I could even hear them sneering and hissing. I turned and ran all the way back to Jon's house. It was a very intense experience that is engraved into my memory forever.

WHAT DISCERNING OF SPIRITS IS NOT

It is not the gift of Criticism

Many people claim no responsibility for their criticism of others, under the guise of saying that they "discern such and such." The truth is that we are always responsible for our words because *"out of the overflow of the heart, the mouth speaks"* (Matt. 12:34). If we are gossiping, backbiting, dishonoring, or smearing anyone, we need to stop and repent. Be careful not to make discerning of spirits an ugly thing to others by misrepresenting it in this way. Typically, when criticism and complaining about others is taking place, discernment is not in action. Where there is a lack of prayer, complaining will fill that void.

If we are going to look at people through Jesus' eyes, then we can't be carrying a record of wrongs and suspecting wrong of others.

It is not the gift of Suspicion

Whether out of emotional wounds or a bad past experience with an individual, we can easily slip into suspicion. First Corinthians 13:5 says, *"Love keeps no record of wrongs."* Most often suspicion is built upon a record of some sort, whether from firsthand experience or second-hand gossip from someone else. If we are going to look at people through Jesus' eyes, then we can't be carrying a record of wrongs and suspecting wrong of others. Please—for your own sake and for clear discernment, forgive the record and repent for having held it.

It is not the gift of Manipulation

This is a question of motives. When someone says, "I discern that you should such and such." It carries more weight than if someone just gives you his or her opinion. If they are not really listening to the Holy Spirit and speaking out of discernment, then they are actually using the Lord's name in vain. My definition of using the Lord's name in vain is putting the weight of *"God said"* behind anything He didn't actually say.

This also happens frequently with the gift of prophecy. Unfortunately, people who don't feel that they will be listened to, will sometimes make it seem like the Lord gave them a "word" or "discernment." This is dangerous ground to be on. These gifts are not to be used to control or manipulate others. The gifts are to be used to build up the Church (see 1 Cor. 12:7) not to tear her down.

It is not the gift of Condemnation

Romans 8:1 says, *"There is now no condemnation for those who are in Christ Jesus."* I would say that since there is no condemnation for us, then we should have none in us to give to others. We are not carriers of condemnation—we see the world through Jesus' eyes and He is the one who said that He did not come to condemn the world. *"For God did not send his Son into the world to condemn the world, but to save the world through him"* (John 3:17). It is never the job of a Christian to condemn.

It is not, "only a deliverance tool"

This is a common misunderstanding. Many in the church have been taught to relegate the gift of discerning of spirits to deliverance ministry only. I believe that this has caused the gift to be minimized and ignored.

The truth is that this gift picks up on four different categories of spirits, only one of them being the demonic. We are in great need of this gift in all four areas and to say that it only relates to deliverance is wasteful.

What if I truly discern something negative about someone?

It is true that a small percentage of discerning of spirits will discern the sinful or negative parts of other individuals. We must properly process this information, in no way should this information turn into slander. The only reason the Holy Spirit is entrusting it to you is so that you can either pray on their behalf or bring them into healing (Gal 6:1, 2). The best example of this is in the story of Jesus speaking to the Samaritan woman at the well in John 4. He did not bring condemnation, just pure love. He spoke directly to her. He in no way slandered her to others.

He did not bring condemnation, just pure love.

"He told her, "Go, call your husband and come back." "I have no husband," she replied. Jesus said to her, "You are right when you say you have no husband. The fact is, you have had five husbands, and the man you now have is not your husband. What you have just said is quite true." "Sir," the woman said, "I can see that you are a prophet" (John 4:16-19).

FIVE FILTERS

How do we work with our discernment to determine the good from the bad? To answer that question, we will look at five filters that can help us understand what our discernment is telling us.

1. Agreement With Scripture

Since there are so many false teachings, personal opinions, and just plain bad theologies that exist, how do we know what is right from what is wrong? The Bible is immovable, unchanging truth, and everything else has to be compared against the Word. No matter what anyone else teaches, we have the more accurate Word of God according to Second Peter 1:19:

And so we have the prophetic word confirmed, which you do well to heed as a light that shines in a dark place, until the day dawns and the morning star rises in your hearts (NKJV).

And the words of the LORD are flawless, like silver refined in a furnace of clay, purified seven times. (Psalm 12:6).

2. Look at the Outward Fruit of the Source

*Watch out for false prophets. They come to you in sheep's clothing, but inwardly they are ferocious wolves. **By their fruit you will recognize them.** Do people pick grapes from thorn bushes, or figs from thistles?* (Matthew 7:15-16).

If the fruit is the same in nature as the fruit of the Spirit, then perhaps God is the source. Galatians 5:22-23 tells us the nature of God's fruit:

But the fruit of the Spirit is love, joy, peace, patience, kindness, goodness, faithfulness, gentleness and self-control. Against such things there is no law.

3. The Anointing of the Holy Spirit, Which Will Guide Us Toward the Truth

But you have an anointing from the Holy One, and all of you know the truth....I am writing these things to you about those who are trying to lead you astray. As for you, the anointing you received from Him remains in you, and you do not need anyone to teach you. But as His anointing teaches you about all things and as that anointing is real, not counterfeit—just as it has taught you, remain in Him. (1 John 2:20, 26-27).

These verses could be confused as a contradiction of Ephesians 4:11-13 where Paul set in place the role of a teacher, but this is just not the case.

In practical terms, if two teachers who are equally equipped to handle the Word are teaching two opposite views, the anointing of the Holy Spirit can guide you towards the truth of the right view. I would add a caution that with any of these filters, you may have a personal hindrance to the filter working properly. Perhaps you were raised in a church that taught you something that was wrong. When you hear the truth preached, you may not be able to filter correctly because of your past doctrine. Ultimately, if your discernment is going to be supernatural, you have to be humble enough to let the Holy Spirit change, guide, and direct you.

4. Obeying the Peace of Christ in Your Heart

Let the peace of Christ rule in your hearts, since as members of one body you were called to peace. And be thankful (Colossians 3:15).

Interestingly, the root word for "rule" in this verse is the same root word from which we get our word *umpire*. In baseball the umpire is the closest official to the home plate; therefore, he is the best person to make an impartial judgment call. He is the one person who has the authority to decide if a player is "safe" or "out."

In a similar manner, when we have a choice or decision in front of us, the indwelling peace of Christ in our heart will help guide us. If you are tempted, the peace of Christ within you will be disturbed. If you are going to make the right decision, even though it is a scary step of faith, the peace of Christ will increase your confidence. When you are faced with a situation, you should pause for a moment and take stock of the condition of your peace. Let the Holy Spirit tell you if you are "safe" or if you are "out."

Take stock of the condition of your peace.

5. The Ways and Nature of God

If you look at the nature of God, there are many things that are easy to filter. It is not in God's nature to approve of abortion, murder, homosexuality, adultery, stealing, lying, witchcraft, disease, injustice, etc. The Bible is our basis for understanding the nature of God. By setting aside opinions and bias, answers can be found in the Word about everything in the nature and ways of God.

Passages like this one show us so much about the ways and nature of God:

Bless the Lord, O my soul, and forget not all His benefits: who forgives all your iniquities, who heals all your diseases, who redeems your life from destruction, who crowns you with loving-kindness and tender mercies, who satisfies your mouth with good things, so that your youth is renewed like the eagle's. The Lord executes righteousness and justice for all who are oppressed. He made known His ways to Moses, His acts to the children of Israel (Psalm 103:2-7 NKJV).

FINAL WORD ABOUT FILTERS

There are many voices in the world which are clamoring for your attention. It is so important to have a system to filter through the voices that you are hearing. We want to be able to know clearly that we are hearing the voice of the Lord and not being deceived by the voice of another. I picture this process of filtering as if I have a handful of mud, and I only want the water. If I were to take a window screen and mash my handful of mud against it, then I would prevent some of the mud from getting through, but much of it would still get through. The best plan of action would be to place multiple window screens, say five for example, in layers over each other, then mash the mud against them. I would then get mostly water. This is how I imagine that these filters work for us.

ACTIVATION

This exercise may take some time. Start by getting a sheet of paper and a writing implement. Now write a letter from Jesus to yourself. Jesus abides within you, so all you have to do is focus on listening to Him speak to you and write a letter of what He says.

The Scripture tells us that all prophetic words are to be tested and proven. The next step is to examine the letter under each filter to be sure that every sentence lines up with the filters. If a filter is violated, scratch out that sentence from your letter. This is a good practice for what you should do with each prophetic word that you receive and each word that you believe that you are hearing from the Lord.

Go back to Activation II from Chapter 6, "The Unseen Realm," and apply the five filters to your letter. Then deliver this letter of love and encouragement to that individual. Whether you have to call, mail, or deliver in person, do not underestimate the value of giving this to the other person. It is not only good for growing your personal gifting, but I have found many people who I have given letters to who have come back to me years later and told me that they still carry that letter in their backpack or purse and read it regularly. This exercise can be done regularly and will continue to grow and stretch your faith and gifting, and you will be leaving a trail of blessing others behind you as you do it.

ENDNOTES

1. Daniel Goleman, *Emotional Intelligence: Why It Can Matter More Than IQ* (New York, NY: Bantam Books, 1995).

2. This information comes from W. E. Vine and F. F. Bruce, *Vine's Expository Dictionary of Old and New Testament Words* (Old Tappan, NJ: Fleming H. Revell Company, 1981), 314, 315, 222.

Hindrances to Discernment

There are many things that can hinder us from operating clearly in discerning of spirits. We should be protective of what we allow our eyes to see and our ears to hear. There are things that can violate us spiritually. We must also watch over our heart and motives so that our ability to discern is not distorted. The following categories are just a sampling of the most common things that distort discernment.

SCARY MOVIES

Movies can powerfully stir the imagination. As those who want to operate in the highest level of accuracy in discerning of spirits, we have to be careful of the food that we feed our imagination. There are hundreds of wonderful movies, and they can be a great way to relax and unwind after a long day, but there are also very evil movies.

I first realized the power of scary movies when I saw "Signs" with Mel Gibson.

Movies that are intended to scare, cause fear, and keep you in constant suspense can be very influential on your discernment. As for which movies this would apply to, I believe it is person specific, not a legalistic rule imposed by others. For example, I first realized the power of scary movies when I saw *Signs* with Mel Gibson. To most people this was not a scary movie. I, however, had recently received a powerful impartation that had caused my discernment to be heightened, and as a result I had some scary encounters with the demonic after watching this movie. When a film is watched for enjoyment, our spirit is open and can receive defilement that we did not intend to receive.

However, I have no problem watching such movies as *The Exorcism of Emily Rose*, because as a minister, I want to be aware of what is influencing America's understanding of deliverance. When I watch such a film, I watch it as research and I have my heart guarded. My standards are personal, and I would recommend that you prayerfully consider which movies you need to avoid. Fear-inducing movies will hinder your discernment.

PAST EMOTIONAL WOUNDS

As humans living in a fallen world, we tend to carry around a lot of emotional "baggage." We can pick up baggage from family, friends, coworkers, and church leaders. This baggage can cause our discernment to be inaccurate. Let us make sure that our heart is the same as Jesus toward those around us. If anything is preventing you from loving someone the same way Jesus loves them, you may need to repent or forgive.

Consider the emotional response of James and John when they wanted to call down fire upon the Samaritan village (see Luke 9:54-56). Jesus very specifically told them that they didn't realize what spirit they were operating under. This can happen very easily—one moment your discernment is sharp; then suddenly a personal wound causes discernment to be far from accurate.

Practically speaking, this happens when there is a room full of people and there is a person present from whom you received a personal wound. The presence of this one person can cause interference in your ability to operate with the heart of the Lord. The best remedy is to deal with your hurts, offenses, and wounds by extending forgiveness. You will know when you have truly forgiven someone, if, when you look at them, you have compassion for them in your heart. The healthier you are emotionally, the healthier your discerning ability will be.

BAD DOCTRINE

The presence of bad teaching can drastically limit your ability to operate in discerning of spirits. If you have been taught that you don't have authority over the demonic, you may be too afraid to use discernment. Perhaps you have been taught that it is not your gift and it is unavailable to you. Maybe you had been trained in the occult or New Age before you became a believer. These can all be hindrances to operating fully and correctly in discerning of spirits. The best idea is to find excellent, biblically based teaching to clarify and improve your under-standing.[1] Always remember to remain humble enough in your beliefs that the Holy Spirit can gently correct or guide you to greater truth. Someone once said, "Bad doctrine is like bad breath; you are usually the last one to know you have it, and no one wants to tell you."

INTERNAL STRESS

The stress of work, family, lack of sleep, health issues, finances, deferred hopes, and a host of other issues can interfere with our discernment. We must have an up-to-date, abiding relationship with Jesus to handle stress correctly. We must operate out of a heart of peace. Without this, we will be inaccurate in our discernment gift.

We must operate out of a heart of peace.

"Do not be anxious about anything, but in everything, by prayer and petition, with thanksgiving, present your requests to God" (Philippians 4:6).

THE FEAR OF MAN

"The fear of man will prove to be a snare, but whoever trusts in the Lord is kept safe" (Proverbs 29:25).

The only thing that we are allowed to fear as Christians is God Himself. If we are afraid of man or man's opinion, it will hinder our ability to discern accurately.

"Does Job fear God for nothing?" satan replied. "Have You not put a hedge around him and his household and everything he has? You have blessed the work of his hands, so that his flocks and herds are spread throughout the land" (Job 1:9-10).

The principle is this, *"What you fear will hedge you in."* If you fear the devil, he will hedge you in. If you fear the Lord, He will put His hedge of protection around you. This same principle can also hedge in your ability to discern correctly. Fear only the Lord, and let Him hedge you in. Entrust yourself to Him fully; cast all your cares on Him for He cares for you (see 1 Pet. 5:7).

Evil Motives

Your motives can taint your gift. Jesus rebuked Peter about his heart motives:

But when Jesus turned and looked at His disciples, He rebuked Peter. "Get behind Me, satan!" He said. "You do not have in mind the things of God, but the things of men" (Mark 8:33).

Jesus also rebuked James and John for not having a right heart.

"And He sent messengers on ahead, who went into a Samaritan village to get things ready for Him; but the people there did not welcome Him, because He was heading for Jerusalem. When the disciples James and John saw this, they asked, "Lord, do you want us to call fire down from heaven to destroy them?" But Jesus turned and rebuked them" (Luke 9:52-55).

Apparently, Peter learned his lesson from Jesus about having right motives. Peter later rebuked Simon the sorcerer in Acts 8, because he had evil motives in his heart. After Peter had learned his lesson from Jesus about heart motives, he was then equipped to correct others.

When Simon saw that the Spirit was given at the laying on of the apostles' hands, he offered them money and said, "Give me also this ability so that everyone on whom I lay my hands may receive the Holy Spirit."

Peter answered: "May your money perish with you, because you thought you could buy the gift of God with money! You have no part or share in this ministry, because your heart is not right before God. Repent of this wickedness and pray to the Lord. Perhaps He will forgive you for having such a thought in your heart. For I see that you are full of bitterness and captive to sin." Then Simon answered, "Pray to the Lord for me so that nothing you have said may happen to me" (Acts 8:18-24).

We have to be careful that our operation of the gifts is used in selfless love, not out of some form of self-promotion or financial gain.

Superstition

*...with whom the Lord had made a covenant and charged them, saying: "**You shall not fear other gods**...[and again]...**you shall not fear other gods**. And the covenant that I have made with you, you shall not forget, **nor shall you fear other gods**"* (2 Kings 17:35-38 NKJV).

There are far too many Christians today who think they are spiritual because they can "sense" the presence of evil spirits, or "discern territorial demons." It is good that we can discern the presence of something evil, but what many have done with the information has bordered on superstition.

Jesus finished out His 40-day fast (see Matthew 4) with a face-to-face visitation by satan himself, yet we don't see any fear on the part of Jesus. No spookiness, no nonsense—He just stood in His personal identity, as we should, and rebuked the devil out of Scripture as we should. There are many Christians today who have become so spooky spiritually that they do not stand in the confidence of their identity.

LUST ISSUES

"You have heard that it was said, 'Do not commit adultery.' But I tell you that anyone who looks at a woman lustfully has already committed adultery with her in his heart" (Matthew 5:27-28).

The vast proliferation of pornography, especially through the Internet, is the enemy's plan to pollute our eyes spiritually. He is more aware than the Church is that the Lord intends to raise up the gift of discerning of spirits throughout His Body in the earth.

God is bringing restoration to discernment.

The Body of Christ has been blind to the spirit realm around us for too long, and God is bringing restoration to discernment. The enemy would like to entrap the Church in a sinful bondage to lust, thus preempting the Lord's restoration. (If you are struggling in this arena, I would strongly recommend reading Eyes of Honor.)

ACTIVATION

Jesus said,

"The eye is the lamp of the body. If your eyes are good, your whole body will be full of light. But if your eyes are bad, your whole body will be full of darkness. If then the light within you is darkness, how great is that darkness!" (Matthew 6:22-23).

And Psalm 101:3 says, *"I will set before my eyes no vile thing."*

Many of us have darkened our spiritual eyes with the filth of sin. Put the following prayer in your own words to cleanse your spiritual eyes.

Lord Jesus,

I confess that I have put certain things in my sight and hearing that are sinful. I ask for Your forgiveness and cleansing. I forgive any individuals who have hurt or offended me [include their names and be specific about what they did]. Wash my eyes clean and give Me your grace to walk in freedom and wholeness.

As a prophetic act of cleansing, splash running water over your eyes.

ENDNOTE

1. I recommend my book, *Normal Christianity*, (Shippensburg, PA: Destiny Image Publishers, 2011).

CHAPTER 10

The Force of Love

WHY A CHAPTER ON LOVE?

When we look at the apostle Paul's first letter to the Corinthians, we must remember that it is a letter, not a book with chapters. The thoughts throughout the whole letter are actually connected and build on one another. In our world of chapters, verses, and endless Bible versions, it is easy to forget the original fluidity of Paul's letters.

Remembering that the letter was not divided into chapters originally, we will focus on chapters 12 to 14, specifically.

- Chapter 12 contains the list of the nine spiritual gifts.

- Chapter 13 is the "love chapter."

- Chapter 14 explains the application of the spiritual gifts in the church congregation.

What we often fail to recognize is that Chapter 13 is in between 12 and 14 on purpose. Every spiritual gift has to be used in love, *"whether you speak in the tongue of men or angels, or have the gift of prophecy, or can fathom all mysteries"* (see 1 Cor. 13:1-2). This is why the "love chapter" is in the middle of the discussion of the gifts.

The gifts have to operate through love.

The gifts have to operate through love. Many people have a wimpy understanding of love, or they lean the other way into a harsh understanding of so-called "tough love."

I recommend the following as a guide. Discerning of spirits is looking at anything in life through the eyes of Jesus. It is like putting on a pair of glasses that would enable you to see people and situations as if you were looking through Jesus' eyes. Jesus looks at everything through a lens of perfect love. If you want to know when discerning of spirits is not in operation, remember this definition.

What Is Love?

One of the most well-known sections of Scripture is First Corinthians 13. It is frequently spoken at weddings all over the country. The fact is, First Corinthians 13:4-8 gives one of the best definitions of love that has ever been written. This passage gives 16 key points about what love is: *(1) patient, (2) kind, (3) does not envy, (4) does not boast, (5) is not proud, (6) is not rude, (7) is not self-seeking, (8) is not easily angered, (9) keeps no record of wrongs, (10) does not delight in evil, (11) rejoices with the truth, (12) always protects, (13) always trusts, (14) always hopes, (15) always perseveres, (16) never fails.*

We have another definition of love in Galatians that many have overlooked. When we refer to the fruit of the spirit mentioned in Galatians 5, often the thinking is that this is a list of character traits. The passage starts with verse 22 saying, *"But the fruit of the spirit is love..."* Notice that the fruit is singular. If you look in the original language of the text, the fruit of the spirit is truly singular, it is not the fruit(s) of the spirit. Love is the one fruit of the spirit. The eight words that come after, *"... joy, peace, patience, kindness, goodness, faithfulness, gentleness and self-control"* are merely further descriptions of the one fruit of the spirit. In other words, love is full of joy, full of peace, full of kindness, and so on.

Many have a weak notion of love as simply a feeling. A closer look at the Word shows us that love is a choice. God so loved the world, that He made the choice to do something (see John 3:16). We need to choose to walk in the lifestyle of love. The following three verses make it very clear that love is a decision:

> *"But since we belong to the day, let us be self-controlled, **putting on faith and love** as a breastplate, and the hope of salvation as a helmet"* (1 Thessalonians 5:8).

> *"But you, man of God, flee from all this, and **pursue...love..."** (1 Timothy 6:11).

> *"Flee the evil desires of youth, and **pursue...love**...along with those who call on the Lord out of a pure heart"* (2 Timothy 2:22).

Love is not only a choice that is made once, but it is a choice that we make daily. We should be known for having our whole lifestyle revolve around love. It is the filter that all of our words, attitudes, and actions have to go through before we speak or act.

*"As you have heard from the beginning, His command is that you **walk in love**"* (2 John 1:6b).

*"...**live a life of love,** just as Christ loved us and gave Himself up for us as a fragrant offering and sacrifice to God"* (Ephesians 5:2).

"Keep yourselves in God's love..." (Jude 1:21).

"Let all that you do be done with love" (1 Corinthians 16:14 NKJV).

Love has a certain way that it treats others. As we have seen, it is kind, patient, gentle, keeps no record of wrongs, etc. Love also has a unique quality about it, in that it can cover sin: *"Above all, love each other deeply, because love covers over a multitude of sins"* (1 Pet. 4:8).

We are called to love each other deeply.

We are called to love each other deeply, and many have been hindered from doing that because sin has been left exposed. Sin needs to be repented of, forgiven, and the record destroyed. Without love, we will still see each other through the lens of that past violation. Love literally gives us back the eyes to see each other without the sin.

Even in the cases where confrontation and exposure are needed to deal with sin, we have a model for how to handle that. The truth must be spoken in love. This pertains to our motivations. We are not to speak the truth just to validate ourselves; we don't speak the truth to injure others; we speak the truth out of a heart of love—a heart that desires healing and restoration: *"...speak the truth in love..."* (see Eph. 4:15a).

*"Therefore, as God's chosen people, holy and dearly loved, clothe yourselves with compassion, kindness, humility, gentleness and patience. And **over all these virtues put on love,** which binds them all together in perfect unity"* (Colossians 3:12,14).

Love is put in the chief place above all other virtues in Scripture. It is of the utmost importance. Not only is it the number one priority, but it also is the glue that holds all the other virtues in perfect balance. It would be easy for someone whose highest value is courage to mistreat others. But courage will function at its optimum capacity when used under love.

Love is as powerful as two evil forces in the world, fear and death. Song of Songs 8:6 says that love is as strong as death, and First John says that there is no fear in love: *"There is no fear in love; but perfect love casts out fear, because fear involves torment. But he who fears has not been made perfect in love"* (1 John 4:18 NKJV).

Love is literally a force in the spirit realm. It is as strong as death, and perfect love casts out fear. Many in the Church have pursued greater faith, but even faith does not function correctly without love: *"...faith works through love"* (see Gal. 5:6b NKJV).

Speaking of faith, Jesus said, *"I tell you the truth, if you have faith as small as a mustard seed, you can say to this mountain, 'Move from here to there' and it will move. Nothing will be impossible for you"* (Matt. 17:20b; see also Luke 17:6).

Faith has a power or force great enough to move a mountain; now consider the following truth: *"And now these three remain: faith, hope and love. But **the greatest of these is love"*** (1 Cor. 13:13).

What if we lived our life with even a mustard seed of love?

This is an amazing statement: Love is a greater force than hope or even faith. Thousands of sermons and books have been written about the incredible power of faith, but the even greater power of love has not received as much focus. If a mustard seed of faith can move a mountain or uproot and cast a tree into the sea, then what kind of magnificent power dwells in love? What if we lived our life with even a mustard seed of love? It would be way beyond moving mountains. This is the realm that I believe God is calling the Church worldwide to step into.

And I pray that you, being rooted and established in love, may have power, together with all the saints, to grasp how wide and long and high and deep is the love of Christ, and to know this love that surpasses knowledge—that you may be filled to the measure of all the fullness of God (Ephesians 3:17b-19).

This builds on our previous thought about love being greater than faith. Only by grasping and being firmly rooted in love can we be filled with all the fullness of God. Like Ephesians 3 says, *"the love of Christ...surpasses knowledge."*

What would "being filled with the fullness of God" look like? I would say that it would be the purest form of being like Jesus. Because the Word says, *"God was pleased to have all His fullness dwell in Him* [Jesus]*"* (Col. 1:19).

Unconditional Love

We have probably all heard the term *unconditional love.* As Christians, we should have the best understanding of what this phrase means because Jesus is the only person who has ever perfectly demonstrated unconditional love. When the word *unconditional* is used, it is referring to how we as humans typically set parameters for our relationships, such as, "If you do this, then I will respond in this manner." Jesus broke the transactional nature of relationships by requiring nothing of us. He did not ask anything from us when we were lost in sin. As John 3:16 says, *"For God so loved the world that He sent His one and only Son, that whoever believes in Him shall not perish but have eternal life."*

God did not ask you to do anything before He would love you; without conditions, He chose to love us and act in love toward us. The apostle Paul reiterates this point in Romans 5:6-8: *"You see, at just the right time, when we were still powerless, Christ died for the ungodly. Very rarely will anyone die for a righteous man, though for a good man someone might possibly dare to die. But God demonstrates His own love for us in this: While we were still sinners, Christ died for us."*

God did not ask you to do anything before He would love you.

Unconditional love is a kind of love that is hard to grasp as a human. Many people spend their life trying to live and act in such a way that they will be acceptable to others, yet Jesus (God the Father and the Holy Spirit included) loves us without condition. Ephesians 3:19 says that this love *"surpasses knowledge,"* and Romans

8:39 says that nothing can separate us from the *"love of God that is in Christ Jesus our Lord."*

INCREASING THE FORCE OF LOVE

The next logical thought would be, "How can I have more of this love in my life?"

I would like to share a great story that Kenneth Hagin Sr. wrote, which illustrates an important point about growing in love.

I was holding a meeting one time, and three pastors came to visit my services. After the meeting, we all went out to eat and fellowship together. These pastors began talking about the subject of the love of God. I was just listening to their conversation. I wasn't talking much. You know, sometimes you can learn more by listening than you can by talking because you already know everything *you* know!

Anyway, these pastors got to talking about how much believers fail in the love walk. And one of the pastors spoke up and said, "I'll tell you what! We need to pray! We need to pray that God would give us love. We just don't have the love of God as we ought to have."

I didn't say anything. But I thought to myself, "Since the love of God has been shed abroad in our hearts, then if a person doesn't seem to have love, he's just got to learn to walk in the light of what he already has. That's where the problem is." (See Rom. 5:5.)

Finally, one of the pastors asked me, "Brother Hagin, what do you think about it?" I asked, "Do you really want to know?" "Yes!" he said. "Well, if you fellows don't have any love, as you just got through saying, then you need to get saved!" They looked at me in astonishment—sort of like I'd slapped them with a wet dish rag.

I continued, "The way you talk, we don't have the love of God. But the Bible says, *'We know that we have passed from death to life, because we love the brethren.'* And if we're saved, we've got the love of God in our hearts because the Bible says *the love of God has been shed abroad in our hearts by the Holy Ghost"* (1 John 3:14 NKJV; Rom. 5:5 KJV).

"It's not a matter of needing to pray that God would send us love, because He's already given every believer a measure of love, just like He's already given every believer a measure of faith. It's just a matter of stirring up and using what's already on the inside!"

I said, "If you're saved, you already have a measure of love. You can pray until you are blue in the face that God would give you more love, but the love you have will never be increased until you feed it on God's Word and exercise it so it can develop.

If you're saved, you already have a measure of love.

"If you develop it, then it will be increased. Feeding it on the Word and exercising it is the way you increase love. Love has to be exercised before it will produce results. But if you will be faithful to exercise love, it will produce great fruit"[1]

HOW DO WE WALK IN THE LOVE THAT WAS POURED INTO OUR HEARTS?

*"And so we **know and rely on the love God has for us.** God is love. **Whoever lives in love** lives in God, and God in him. In this way, love is made complete among us so that we will have confidence on the day of judgment, because in this world we are like Him"* (1 John 4:16-17).

First, we must acknowledge and have confidence that God loves us. And second, we must live our life pouring out that love to others. Many Christians try to walk in love toward others, without a constant acknowledgment of the love God has toward them. When you keep your focus on the love God has for you, then you overflow with that love toward others.

WITHOUT LOVE THERE IS NO DISCERNMENT

"Follow the way of love and eagerly desire spiritual gifts, especially the gift of prophecy" (1 Corinthians 14:1).

I have found that you have to have the foundation of "following the way of love" before the gifts that you "eagerly desire" will function correctly. You may be able to see some limited operation of the gifts without walking in love, but ultimately they will be missing the heart of God.

WHEN LOVE LEAVES, SO DOES DISCERNMENT

I personally have a hard time operating in the gifts when I am not walking in love. For example, if someone with a difficult personality is in the vicinity and I am trying to focus my discernment, I run into a problem. My spirit is troubled by the difficult individual, and I am not able to step into love and function properly. I am trying to aim my love toward one person, while my discernment is picking up my bad attitude toward the other. I am literally getting in my own way.

LOVE IS DISCERNABLE

"By this all men will know that you are My disciples, if you love one another" (John 13:35).

While it is true that having a faith so powerful that it can move mountains is a sign that someone is walking under God's favor and anointing, the trait that Jesus established to discern one of His disciples is love.

ACTIVATION

"And so we know and rely on the love God has for us. God is love. Whoever lives in love lives in God, and God in him" (1 John 4:16).

Close your eyes and engage your imagination. Focus on the fact that God has shed His love abroad in your heart. Recall to your mind that you rely on God's love. Acknowledge the love that is within you. Picture it welling up, healing every wound, bringing freedom, healing your memories. The truth of God's love for you, and in you, will set you free. This love gives your eyes the ability to see the world through the eyes of Jesus.

Picture the people in your life who you need to forgive—the ones who have hurt you—and see them through these eyes of love and forgive them. Take 5 to 10 minutes right now and give it to the Lord. Focus on the love of Jesus and meditate on these truths.

ENDNOTE

1. Kenneth Hagin, *Love, the Way to Victory* (Tulsa, OK: Faith Library Pub., 1994), 25-27.

—Part Three—

Unlocking
the Gift

CHAPTER 11

Four Keys to Increasing Faith

The Lord showed me a picture of a long hallway with doors on both sides, like you might see in a hotel. Each door had the name of a biblical experience on it. The first door said on it, "The door of salvation." The next door said on it, "The door of baptism in the Holy Spirit." There were endless doors, each with different labels such as, "The door of healing," or "The door of deliverance."

Each one of these doors had a lock. In order to access these experiences, you needed a key. The Lord showed me that one key will open all these doors, and that key is faith. Even though the Word is filled with promises and truths, the key of faith is required to open every door of promise.

Faith should always lead us into an experience of what we are having faith for. If I have faith for salvation, I should experience salvation. If I have faith for baptism in the Holy Spirit, I should experience baptism in the Holy Spirit. Every promise in Scripture is experienced by faith. Faith is the key that unlocks every door to experiences. *"Therefore I tell you, whatever you ask for in prayer, believe that you have received it, and it will be yours"* (Mark 11:24). Faith brings us into an experience.

Scripture is filled with promises of what can be received and walked in by faith. Looking at Hebrews 11, which has been nicknamed "The Hall of Faith," each person mentioned had an experience with God, and each story was remembered as by faith. The key to their experience was that they entered in by faith. If we want to experience greater discernment, we will need greater faith. This requires not just mental agreement, but an active faith that turns the key in the doorknob. I can say in my mind that I believe God can heal me, but if I don't have an active faith, then I will lack the experience.

Doors of Experience

These are ten examples of truth that can be realized, felt, lived, enjoyed, and experienced in life by faith.

1. **Salvation**—We are saved by grace, through faith (see Eph. 2:8).

2. **Healing**—By His stripes, we are healed (see Isa. 53:3-5; 1 Pet. 2:24).

3. **Abiding**—We are with Christ hidden in God (see Col. 3:1-3).

4. **Insight**—We have the mind of Christ (see 1 Cor. 2:16).

5. **Power**—Your will be done on earth as it is in Heaven (see Matt. 6:10).

6. **Joy**—In His presence is fullness of joy (see Ps. 16:11).

7. **Authority**—We are seated with Him in heavenly places (see Eph. 2:1-10).

8. **Hearing God**—My sheep hear My voice (see John 10:27).

9. **Fruit of the Spirit**—Since we live in the Spirit, let us walk in the Spirit (see Gal. 5:22-25).

10. **Intimacy**—Those joined with the Lord are one spirit with Him (see 1 Cor. 6:17).

By now you might be thinking that this is good, but what does it have to do with seeing into the spirit? The connection is that *"we walk by faith, not by sight"* (2 Cor. 5:7 NKJV). Faith is what enables our spirit eyes. Faith helps us see the unseen. We do not make spiritual decisions by what can be seen with physical eyes. Faith reads the Word and sees the angels who surround us. Faith sees the presence of Jesus each day, as He said, "I will never leave you nor forsake you." Most people are content hearing these truths and standing outside the door of truth, never entering in. Faith cannot be satisfied with the mental knowledge of truth. Faith is only satisfied when one enters into truth.

It must be remembered that the Word of God is living and active. It is alive and waiting for you to experience its glorious riches. Experiencing angels, Heaven, the manifest presence of God, visions, trances, and dreams are available to us through faith. I will put one caution here for balance. You can't take a Scripture and wield it without the direction of the Holy Spirit. Remember, the Word of God is the sword of the spirit, which means it is the Holy Spirit's sword, not your sword. We need to submit to the Holy Spirit for its wielding to be safe and powerful.

STEP INSIDE

Many of us have stepped through the doors of salvation, baptism in the Holy Spirit, healing, deliverance, and hearing the voice of God, and have had these experiences. This is about as far down the hallway of experience as the Western Church has been willing to venture.

These are the doors that are commonly preached about, believed in, and entered into. Yet the Scripture is not exhausted by these few wonderful experiences alone. God has given us a whole book of truths to enter into, and none of us will ever exhaust all that can be experienced through faith.

God has given us a whole book
of truths to enter into.

Have we yet experienced to the fullest what it means to be "in Christ," or "seated in heavenly places," or being "one spirit with Him," or "walking in the spirit," or "having the mind of Christ"? Let me encourage you; there is so much more! Keep pushing down the hallway.

SOME DOORS ARE HARDER TO OPEN

The door of salvation has been in active use and teaching for centuries. Martin Luther was a pioneer in pushing this door open for the Body of Christ. Nowadays, salvation by grace through faith is easily experienced.

Now salvation is taught in every true church and can be brought with confidence to anyone, anytime, even to a homeless person on the street or a rich person on Wall Street. Yet, some of the doors seem harder to experience. Prophecy, for example. Perhaps I have faith to believe, *"My sheep can hear My voice,"* but I don't always seem to experience hearing His voice.

One explanation could be that some of the infrequently used doors have rust on them, metaphorically speaking, which makes them squeaky and hard to open. This may be why some people still don't get healed or delivered; a certain level of breakthrough has not been obtained and maintained in the Church.

Without Faith, Doors Do Not Open

"For indeed the gospel was preached to us as well as to them; but the word which they heard did not profit them, not being mixed with faith in those who heard it" (Hebrews 4:2).

The Word of God can be negated by the response of the hearer. In this verse, the Word going forth was not lacking, but faith was lacking on the part of certain hearers. Those who heard with faith received the promise, whereas those who heard and did not mix faith with the message received nothing. This concept is summed up in the phrase, "You get out what you put in." If you do not mix faith with the Word of God that you hear, then you will not receive the promises of the Word. God has given you the authority to receive or negate His promises dependent upon your response.

Practical Keys

Experience is what all relationships are made of. If you desire a closer relationship with God, then your desire includes greater experience with Him. Since we understand that faith leads us to greater experience, we should desire greater faith. Our heart should be the same as the disciples' who said to the Lord, *"Increase our faith!"* (Luke 17:5). Here are four practical keys in the Word that build greater faith.

1. Fasting and Prayer

"Lord, have mercy on my son," he said. "He has seizures and is suffering greatly. He often falls into the fire or into the water. I brought him to Your disciples, but they could not heal him." "O unbelieving and perverse generation," Jesus replied, "how long shall I stay with you? How long shall I put up with you? Bring the boy here to Me."

*Jesus rebuked the demon, and it came out of the boy, and he was healed from that moment. Then the disciples came to Jesus in private and asked, "**Why couldn't we drive it out?**" He replied, "**Because you have so little faith.** I tell you the truth, if you have faith as small as a mustard seed, you can say to this mountain, 'Move from here to there' and it will move. Nothing will be impossible for you." But this kind does not go out except by prayer and fasting* (Matthew 17:15-21).

Jesus says it is because of their little faith, and then He gives them the remedy of prayer with fasting. This will get them the faith they need for the healing and deliverance of the child. Fasting is one of four specific things that we can do to build greater faith. Great faith leads to greater experience.

MORE ABOUT FASTING

Often when I fast, people ask me, "Did God tell you to fast?" I have been considering why people ask that, especially since I commonly respond, "No, He didn't tell me to fast; I just decided to fast." There is nothing that commands us as New Testament believers when to fast, how long to fast, and so on. There were specific times to fast in the Old Testament, but the New Testament does not command us in these things.

The same is true of praying in the Holy Spirit or listening for a "rhema" word from the Lord. The Word tells us that these things will build our faith, but the Lord doesn't command us to activate them; He just makes them available. I believe that each one of these will build our faith, thereby bringing us greater ability to enter experience.

God has given us the tools to build
enough faith to access any door

God has given us the tools to build enough faith to access any door, yet He leaves us our freewill to decide when to fast, when to pray, and when to listen. When we decide to build our faith, it is something we initiate, and then in response He increases our faith so that we can experience more of His Kingdom. This is a fundamental element in our relationship with God; He gives us the choice of the relationship we want: *"Draw near to God, and He will draw near to you"* (James 4:8 NKJV). Another way to say it would be, "The ball is in our court."

2. Praying in the Spirit

"But you, beloved, building yourselves up on your most holy faith, praying in the Holy Spirit" (Jude 1:20 NKJV).

Praying in the Spirit is different from fasting because if you come across a situation where you need to access faith immediately, you can begin praying in the Spirit at a moment's notice. However, fasting is done ahead of time, to store up faith. We can fill ourselves up daily by praying in the Spirit, but it is always on call as well.

3. Hearing the Prophetic Word of God

"So then faith comes by hearing, and hearing by the word [rhema] of God" (Romans 10:17 NKJV).

The "rhema" word of God is when the Lord prophetically applies His words to you, in your situation. He speaks these things directly into your spirit and encourages, strengthens and comforts you. This gives you greater faith. Prophet Bill Hamon says,

A *rhema* is a word or an illustration God speaks directly to us, and it addresses our personal, particular situation. It is a timely, Holy Spirit-inspired Word from the Logos (the Bible) that brings life, power, and faith to perform and fulfill it. Its significance is exemplified in the injunction to take the *"sword of the Spirit, which is the word [rhema] of God"* (Eph. 6:17).

It can be received through others such as by a prophetic word, or be an illumination given to one directly in [his or her] personal meditation time in the Bible or in prayer. The logos is the fixed Word of God—the Scriptures—and the rhema is a particular portion in line with the logos brought forth by the Spirit to be applied directly to something in our personal experience.[1]

4. Fellowshiping with People of Faith

"That you and I may be mutually encouraged by each other's faith" (Romans 1:12b).

Proverbs 27:17 says, *"Iron sharpens iron."* Being around someone who has greater faith than you prods you to greater faith. The encouragement can also come from two equals, who provoke each other to greater faith in the Lord. Personally, I am tremendously encouraged by listening to teachers with great faith, such as Bill Johnson or Heidi Baker. I choose to listen regularly to recordings of their teachings to keep my faith lifted up. I also make conscious decisions to have lunch with people of faith so that we can mutually encourage each other.

"Good Works"

What good is it, my brothers, if a man claims to have faith but has no deeds? Can such faith save him? Suppose a brother or sister is without clothes and daily food. If one of you says to him, "Go, I wish you well; keep warm and well fed," but does nothing about his physical needs, what good is it? In the same way, faith by itself, if it is not accompanied by action, is dead. But someone will say, "You have faith; I have deeds." Show me your faith without deeds, and I will show you my faith by what I do* (James 2:14-18).

I have found that every time I teach on the four keys of faith, I always get a naysayer who comes to warn me after the service. His or her basic premise is that I need to be careful how I teach the four keys because they could be interpreted as a formula of "good works." The implication is that grace and works are mutually exclusive entities.

This is fundamentally not true.

After we have received salvation by grace, good works should flow out of us as a natural byproduct.

After we have received salvation by grace, good works should flow out of us as a natural byproduct. The Book of James implies that an individual's salvation is questionable if good works are not flowing out. Good works are the fruit and evidence of grace and faith.

You foolish man, do you want evidence that faith without deeds is useless? Was not our ancestor Abraham considered righteous for what he did when he offered his son Isaac on the altar? You see that his faith and his actions were working together, and his faith was made complete by what he did. And the scripture was fulfilled that says, "Abraham believed God, and it was credited to him as righteousness," and he was called God's friend. You see that a person is justified by what he does and not by faith alone. In the same way, was not even Rahab the prostitute considered righteous for what she did when she gave lodging to the spies and sent them off in a different direction? As the body without the spirit is dead, so faith without deeds is dead (James 2:20-26).

The four keys are not about good works gaining salvation; the keys only work after salvation is received. Once we have come into the Kingdom there are specific things that we can choose to do to build our confidence and faith substance in the spirit realm (see Heb. 11:1). The keys are just four examples of many things that can be done to strengthen faith. This is not about earning salvation, so the "good works" argument is not applicable.

Faith Is Confidence

There has been a lot of teaching surrounding the word *faith*. Sometimes it can seem like the very definition of the word might be convoluted. I would suggest that we can use another word when we are trying to express ourselves regarding faith.

The word *confidence* is an excellent substitute that the world understands much more clearly. In fact, the word *confidence* can be traced back to two Latin root words, *com-* and *fidere,* which together mean "with faith." So when I speak to a non-Christian on the street and tell them that I have confidence that God wants to save their soul, I am literally saying that I have faith that God wants to save them. Also, when I say that fasting builds my faith, I am saying that it builds my confidence, as does praying in the Spirit, or hearing the prophetic word. This change of terminology will bring much clarity for some of us.

Activation

To build your faith, follow the next four suggestions:

1. Pick a time to fast, perhaps a meal, a day, or a week, then follow through.

2. Make a habit of praying in tongues. Set your watch for three minutes and pray right now.

3. Read the Word until the Holy Spirit lifts a verse off the page to you. This verse may speak to you in an intimate way, or it may seem to have revelation for you. Carry this Word around in your heart all day, and the next day repeat.

4. Call someone who encourages your faith, someone you look up to. Invite them to have lunch with you. Pull on their faith—and be provoked to a greater walk with the Lord. Ask them questions.

ENDNOTES

1. Bill Hamon, *Apostles, Prophets, and the Coming Moves of God* (Santa Rosa Beach, FL: Christian International, 1997), 284-285.

CHAPTER 12

Biblical Meditation

A DIFFERENT KIND OF MEDITATION

The false religions of the world—Hinduism, Buddhism, Islam, and the New Age to name a few—teach that meditation is emptying the mind to have spiritual experiences. This is their understanding of meditation.

The Bible teaches us to meditate in a fundamentally different way—it directs us to meditate on the Word and wait on God. The Bible even tells us what to fill the mind with. In the Word there are five categories on which we are to meditate.

1. Meditate on Good Things

Many people suffer from various mental and emotional illnesses because they only meditate on bad and negative things. Proverbs 23:7 says, *"For as [a man] thinks in his heart, so is he"* (NKJV). We must choose what thoughts we entertain. Because our thoughts influence and change us, they can make or break us; they manifest as the life that we live.

> *"Finally, brethren, whatever things are true, whatever things are noble, whatever things are just, whatever things are pure, whatever things are lovely, whatever things are of good report, if there is any virtue and if there is anything praiseworthy—meditate on these things"* (Philippians 4:8 NKJV).

> *"Let the words of my mouth and the meditation of my heart be acceptable in Your sight, O Lord..."* (Psalms 19:14 NKJV).

> *"May my meditation be sweet to Him; I will be glad in the Lord"* (Psalms 104:34 NKJV).

2. Meditate on the Word of God

The Bible is *"God-breathed and is useful for teaching, rebuking, correcting and training in righteousness, so that the man of God may be thoroughly equipped for every good work"* (2 Tim. 3:16-17). The importance of meditating on the Word is self-evident to many of us. But for good measure, consider Joshua 1:8:

> *"Do not let this Book of the Law depart from your mouth; meditate on it day and night, so that you may be careful to do everything written in it. Then you will be prosperous and successful."*

One of my favorite books of the Bible is Proverbs. When I read it and a verse speaks to me, I repeat it out loud several times. I ponder it, and I chew on it. Then I carry that verse in my heart and mind all day long. It becomes my bread for that day. The next day I open Proverbs again and pull out another piece of bread. If I can find a way to incorporate that word for the day into a conversation with someone, this helps me remember the verse for the future. The true value of Scripture memorization is in application.

3. Meditate on Prophetic Words

There are many things that should be done with prophetic words: testing, judging, proving, warring with, praying over them, and walking them out. One aspect that seems to be under-taught is that we should meditate upon our prophetic words. First Timothy 4:14-15 says, *"Do not neglect the gift that is in you, which was given to you by prophecy with the laying on of the hands of the eldership. Meditate on these things; give yourself entirely to them, that your progress may be evident to all."*

I take this category very seriously. In fact I have a three-ring binder containing sheets of paper on which I have printed all the prophetic words that I have received. I take this with me when I travel; I read it before meetings, after meetings, when I am tired, and so forth. This is a constant source of encouragement, and it keeps my vision focused on the calling of my life. Just as Paul advised Timothy, I give myself to my prophecies.

4. Meditate on the Lord Himself

"When I remember You on my bed, I meditate on You in the night watches" (Ps. 63:6). By keeping our mind focused on the Lord, we encourage our abiding relationship with Him. There are many ways to meditate on the Lord. One of the most practical that I have found is focusing on the names of the Lord. Names equal nature, so by revealing His names to us, God has revealed His nature to us. If He says that His name is, *"Jehovah Rapha, the Lord our healer,"* then He is sharing with you that His nature is that of a healer.

Here are some of the names of the Lord with which to begin your study:

El-Shaddai—The Almighty God (see Gen. 17:1-2)

Jehovah-Jireh—The Lord Our Provider (see Gen. 22:14)

Jehovah-Rapha—The Lord Our Healer (see Exod. 15:22-26)

Jehovah-Tsidqenu—The Lord Our Righteousness (see Jer. 33:16)

Jehovah-Nissi—The Lord Is My Banner (see Exod. 17:15)

Jehovah-Shalom—The Lord Our Peace (see Judg. 6:24)

Jehovah-Shammah—The Lord Is There (see Ezek. 48:35)

Jehovah-Sabaoth—The Lord of Hosts (see Rom. 9:29)

I regularly go on walks around my neighborhood. As I walk, I pray and talk with God. I tell Him everything I am thinking and what is on my heart. At these times the Lord usually reminds me of one of His names. Perhaps I tell Him that I am upset and confused because someone I prayed for didn't get healed. He settles my heart and reminds me that He is Jehovah Rapha, The Lord My Healer. Sometimes while praying I share how weak I am in a certain area, and then I declare, "Lord You are my...(righteousness, healer, provider, etc.—fill in the blank). Meditating on God Himself has been a large part of my prayer life.

5. Meditate on the Works of God

"In the Old Testament the word *testimony* comes from the word, "do again." The implication is that God wants to repeat His wonderful works when we speak of what He has done. In the New Testament we have a confirmation of that principle in Revelation 19:10 *"...the testimony of Jesus is the spirit of prophecy."*[1] This means that when we bring a testimony of the works of God to remembrance, we are actually prophesying that He can do it again now, because *"Jesus Christ is the same yesterday, today, and forever"* (Heb. 13:8).

Meditating on and remembering the works of God are major keys to seeing them repeated. King David understood this well. That is why when he was in a period of suffering he would meditate on God's past works. This not only encouraged David, but it also prophesied into the atmosphere that God could do it again.

"And I said, "This is my anguish; but I will remember the years of the right hand of the Most High." I will remember the works of the Lord; surely I will remember your wonders of old. I will also meditate on all your work, and talk of Your deeds" (Psalms 77:10-12).

"I remember the days of old; I meditate on all Your works; I muse on the work of Your hands" (Psalms 143:5).

It is incredibly important to carry the works of God with you.

It is incredibly important to carry the works of God with you. Some of my favorite conversations are the ones where I can tell a new friend stories of when I have seen God at work. For example, when I recount to a new person my story of how a lemon-sized tumor disappeared under my hand as I prayed, the story reinvigorates my spirit with life. It stirs the Spirit of God within me. When I speak into the atmosphere of something God has done, the atmosphere becomes charged for God to do that same work again, and the faith level rises. Carrying the testimonies of what Jesus has done brings life to dead Christianity. I have found that non-Christians perk up and become interested when I tell the stories of what I have seen God do. Legalism and quoting Scripture without love has turned the world off toward us, but people listen eagerly if we are sharing the stories of the works of God.

THE IMAGINATION IS THE MEDITATION ORGAN OF YOUR SPIRIT

"I pray also that the eyes of your heart may be enlightened in order that you may know the hope to which He has called you, the riches of His glorious inheritance in the saints" (Ephesians 1:18).

If Paul is going to tell the Ephesians that he is praying for them, don't you think he would choose his words carefully? This shows the value that Paul put on receiving enlightenment for the spiritual eyes. The eyes of the heart refer to the human imagination. Clearly this was understood as important in the first century, whereas in the modern Church the imagination has been made a low priority and moved to the fringes of Christendom. In fact people commonly invalidate anything that comes from the imagination with statements like, "Oh that is *just* my imagination." This is unfortunate and we need to stop stifling what God is trying to say to us through our imagination. Adam and Eve had an imagination before the fall of mankind. Therefore, the imagination is not inherently evil. Now that we are believers, we need to take back the realm of the imagination and stop invalidating everything that comes from it. Even Jesus validated the power of the human imagination.

> *You have heard that it was said, "Do not commit adultery." But I tell you that anyone who looks at a woman lustfully has already committed adultery with her in his heart"* (Matthew 5:27-28).

Jesus said that simply using the imagination is as valid as having done it in real life. Understand that if a person sins in the imagination realm, when they step back into the natural realm, they bring back with them the stain of the sin they just committed. The imagination realm releases actual realities in the physical. It is clear that Jesus is speaking of this in a negative context, but in general this validates the power and legitimacy of the imagination. When He says that adultery is committed in the heart, He is referring to the human imagination. This would be an example of using the imagination in meditation in the negative sense. Yet it validates the power and reality of the imagination.

The imagination is the creative organ of your spirit. For example, all inventions in the earth have come from someone's imagination. It has been said that "everything that now exists was once imagined." Even when God determined to create the earth and each person on the earth, He would have imagined first what He was creating. God has quite an imagination!

The imagination is the creative organ of your spirit.

If you are constantly invalidating your imagination while you are awake, then many times God will begin to open your spiritual eyes while you are asleep and dreaming. When the senses of your physical body and soul are at rest, then God is able to bypass any resistance and speak directly to your spirit. *"For God may speak in one way or in another, yet man does not perceive it, in a dream, in a vision of the night, when deep sleep falls upon men, while slumbering on their beds, then He opens the ears of men, and seals their instruction*" (Job 33:14-16 NKJV).

Another author made a great point about invalidating the imagination of children. "What child has not heard something in their room during the night? What youngster has not seen something in the closet? Desiring to comfort their children, but without an appreciation for spiritual encounters, parents inadvertently taught their children that their perceptions were irrational. They turned on the lights to "prove" that nothing was there, or opened the closet door and demonstrated that it was just their imagination.

This is often the beginning of our schooling in Western rationalism, which trains us to doubt our experiences, attributing them to the mere antics of a hyperactive imagination.

It is time to retrain ourselves in the innocent belief of early childhood. When young Samuel heard a voice calling his name in the Temple, Eli did not respond, "You're just hearing things. Look, I will light this oil lamp and prove no one is there. Your imagination is getting the best of you!" Thankfully, Samuel did not have to "undo" bad teaching based on Eli's lack of understanding of the supernatural. This was a great advantage to him on his journey to becoming one of Israel's great prophets[2] (see 1 Sam 3:1-10).

USE YOUR IMAGINATION

The imagination is similar to a television set; it is not essentially good or evil. As with a television, evil can be projected on the imagination, but this does not make the imagination evil. Conversely, Christian and educational programming can be projected on the television, but this doesn't make the television righteous. The television and the imagination are always just conduits.

The imagination is like the television screen, and there is the opportunity to project the things of the flesh or the things of the spirit upon it. The goal is to project on the imagination the righteous things of the spirit. This is done by biblical meditation.

God put an imagination inside every person; it is not a byproduct of the fall of Adam. Adam's imagination is evidenced by his naming all the animals before the fall into sin. We need to be careful that we don't invalidate the voice of our discernment if it comes by way of the imagination. God put your imagination in you, and He is trying to talk to you through it.

EXPERIENCE THE WORD

The goal of operating our imagination through biblical meditation is to enter into an interactive experience.

*"For **the word of God is living and active.** Sharper than any double-edged sword, it penetrates even to dividing soul and spirit, joints and marrow; it judges the thoughts and attitudes of the heart"* (Hebrews 4:12).

Consider carefully what this verse says. It makes an amazing statement that has far-reaching effects. If something is alive and active, then you can interact with it, and it will be responsive and communicate with you. If someone is dead, I can talk to him or her all day, but we won't experience each other. If he or she is alive, then we can talk to each other and interact. If I have a statue of a dog, then I do have a dog, but it is not living and active. This is similar to how many people approach the Word. In reality, the Word is like having a living puppy; it is alive and active, and when you draw near to God, He draws near to you (James 4:8). When I open the Word and am ready to experience it, the Word greets me like a puppy welcoming home his owner. This life and activity that the puppy exhibits gives us a picture of how the Word "jumps" on us and wants us to interact with it.

Jesus also stated that *"The Spirit gives life; the flesh counts for nothing. The words I have spoken to you are spirit and they are life"* (John 6:63). The Word is alive, and it dwells in the spirit because it is spirit. We cannot read the Word only with our fleshly mind; we must engage it in our spirit for it to be properly read. It must be meditated on in our spirit and our imagination.

In John 17:17, Jesus prayed for His disciples: *"Sanctify them by the truth; Your word is truth."* An interesting insight about this verse is that the root word for "truth" can also mean "reality" (Greek: *aletheia*). *Vine's Expository Dictionary* definition of *truth* is "the reality lying at the basis of an appearance; the manifested, veritable, essence of a matter."[3] (I will go into this more in the next chapter.)

Therefore, the Word of God has a reality or realm inside it, and we can enter into the reality of each verse. The Word was given to us so that we can enter into this reality regularly. The Word and the Holy Spirit are our guides in this realm; Jesus said that the Holy Spirit will guide you into all truth.

So, the Holy Spirit is our guide in the reality or realm of the Word. There are countless testimonies of Christians who have had prophetic experiences where they entered into one of these realms of the Word. These should encourage and inspire us to enter in and experience the realities of the Word for ourselves.

HEAVENLY ROOMS

If you are still wondering how you can enter into the realms of the Word, let me share a personal example. I was attending a conference in November 2005, in Harrisburg, Pennsylvania. A friend of mine laid his hand on my chest in prayer, and I had a very powerful reaction. In the physical, it felt like a fire had entered into my chest—it hurt so much I was almost scared. I slumped forward onto the floor, and I entered into a prophetic experience. I came back to my physical awareness two hours later. During this experience, the Lord showed me four different rooms in Heaven.

The first room looked like a warehouse with shelves full of body parts. I sensed that these could be used for people who need physical healing. I believe that when we pray, God already has the parts ready, and somehow He just deposits these into people, and they get healed.

The second room was full of diamonds. When I picked one up and looked closely, I could see the face of a person in each one. I understand this to be the way that Jesus sees each of us. As I turned the diamond in my hand, I could see through it in a new way and see different facets of the person's character. You are literally one of God's gems; He treasures you like a diamond.

The second room was full of diamonds.

The third room was full of paper money of all colors, shapes, and sizes. I sensed that I was looking at a representation of all the types of money in the earth. The Lord was showing me His finance chamber; this was a prophetic vision of "His riches in glory" (Phil. 4:19 NKJV). As He showed me this, He gave me peace that He has all the provision and can always take care of me; this strengthened my faith greatly.

The last room was warm and moist; it seemed round, like being inside a ball. The walls were pink and somewhat flesh-colored. I saw Jesus standing next to me, and I asked Him what this room was. He replied, "This is the reality of Colossians 3:3." I heard the verse resounding in my spirit, *"For you died, and your life is now hidden with Christ in God"* (Col. 3:3). I realized that in the vision I was inside the heart of God the Father, hidden with Christ. I was actually standing inside the heart of God.

This is one example of how we can enter into the realms of the Word. But this is only one verse. I believe that every verse has a prophetic potential, that all of the Word is living and active and ready to engage us, that all of God's Word is truth and has a realm that we can enter into. Now Colossians 3:3 will always have a personal meaning to me because I have experienced it.

Is the Imagination Dangerous?

When we are pursuing the Lord in the person of Jesus Christ, we have no reason to be afraid. Jesus said,

Which of you fathers, if your son asks for a fish, will give him a snake instead? Or if he asks for an egg, will give him a scorpion? If you then, though you are evil, know how to give good gifts to your children, how much more will your Father in heaven give the Holy Spirit to those who ask Him! (Luke 11:11-13).

Yes, it is true that there are scorpions and snakes in the world of the evil imagination. But when we are pursuing God in the Word through the imagination, it would be an insult to the nature of God to be afraid that you are going to receive something dangerous. God is big enough to protect us, and we need not fear. This fear of the imagination stems from a weak view of God and an inaccurate view of the strength of the devil. God wants us to enter in, and He will protect us when we do.

Activation

Use your imagination to engage in meditating on each of the five categories of biblical meditation. I encourage you to activate your spirit and engage in the Word every time you read the Bible; make this a regular practice.

1. Good Things
2. The Word of God (Good visionary passages to start with include the following: Isa. 6; Rev. 1; 4; 22; Ezek. 37; 47; Dan. 10.)

3. Prophetic Words

4. The Lord Himself

5. The Works of God

ENDNOTES

1. Bill Johnson, *Dreaming With God* (Shippensburg, PA: Destiny Image, 2006), 83.

2. Lucas Sherraden, *When Heaven Opens, Discovering the Power of Divine Encounters* (Stafford, TX: Lucas Sherraden Ministries, 2006).

3. W. E. Vine and F. F. Bruce, *Vine's Expository Dictionary of Old and New Testament Words* (Old Tappan, NJ: Fleming H. Revell Co., 1981), 159.

CHAPTER 13

Worship in Spirit and in Truth

I was with 5,000 home group leaders at a church in Manaus, Brazil. The presence of God was incredibly tangible during worship. Then Gary Oates got up to speak, and the presence of the Lord overwhelmed him and knocked him to the floor on the platform. Randy Clark turned to Gary's wife, Kathi, and told her to take over the service. As she took the microphone, she began to prophesy over the nation of Brazil, and a powerful wind began to blow through the church.

Gary Oates described the wind in his own words:

Inside, the wind was whipping around just like on the day of Pentecost—a mighty rushing wind had come into the house.[1]

It blew the potted plants on the stage wildly and even blew open two large arched doors on the stage. While this was happening, I stepped outside the church to see if there was any natural explanation for the wind. Outside, it was eerily calm and peaceful, no wind and no movement. What was happening inside the church was clearly supernatural; the wind was so powerful that it actually blew over a section of 400 empty chairs. Randy got up and called for the ministry team to pray for the sick while the wind continued.

Team members would later talk of strong winds blowing in a circular motion around them as they ministered. Reports would also come back that virtually everyone prayed over that day was instantly healed.[2]

The deaf, in particular, seemed to receive healing. This wind lasted for approximately two hours while we continued to pray for the sick.

Strong worship was a major key in the manifest presence that came down that day.

I believe that exceptionally strong worship was a major key in the manifest presence that came down that day. They had a high level of breakthrough in the realm of worship. There is more in New Testament worship than much of the Church has realized. Jesus brought an incredible shift in worship in the New Testament.

LOCATION IS THE KEY TO WORSHIP

In John 4 we find Jesus sitting at a well talking with a Samaritan woman. Jesus, as always, is not concerned with the cultural taboos that He is violating. Interacting with a Samaritan was a disgrace, and to be interacting with a woman was a double strike. Jesus proceeds to engage her in a discussion about worship. She then brings up a culturally controversial question. Where is the proper place to worship—where the Jews worship or where the Samaritans worship?

> *"Sir," the woman said, "I can see that You are a prophet. Our fathers worshiped on this mountain, but you Jews claim that the place where we must worship is in Jerusalem"* (John 4:19-20).

Jesus, always being one step ahead, gives her a totally unexpected answer. He tells her of a whole new location for proper worship. He says that the place of the Jew's worship and the place of the Samaritan's worship are both being voided, and a new place is being set up.

> *Jesus declared, "Believe me, woman, a time is coming when you will worship the Father neither on this mountain nor in Jerusalem. You Samaritans worship what you do not know; we worship what we do know, for salvation is from the Jews. Yet a time is coming and has now come when the true worshipers will worship the Father in spirit and truth, for they are the kind of worshipers the Father seeks. God is spirit and His worshipers must worship in spirit and in truth."* (John 4:21-24).

This woman's question concerns the location of our worship. Jesus says that the previous locations of worship, whether on this mountain or in Jerusalem, were no longer going to be used. Then He speaks of a new location of worship that was coming in the future. Worship must take place in spirit and in truth. Because God is a spirit, our worship must be in the spirit realm.

We need to recognize the strong imperative of this statement: *"Those who worship Him **must**..."* Our worship is missing a fundamental element unless we gain insight into what the verse is telling us we must do. Take a moment and consider how you have understood this passage in the past or how you have heard it taught. Most people have never been trained to look closely to find out how to properly worship God as a spirit, and yet the key lies right under our nose.

IN SPIRIT AND IN TRUTH

The word *spirit* in John 4:24 could refer to the human spirit, the Holy Spirit, or the spirit realm. In Greek there is one word for spirit (*pneuma*), and it can be difficult to determine which meaning of *spirit* is being conveyed. To determine the meaning of the word *spirit*, we must always look at the context. The best way to do that would be to understand what the word *truth* means.

The prolific author and teacher Watchman Nee gives the following insight into John 4:

> What then is spiritual reality? The Lord said that "God is Spirit, and those who worship Him must worship in spirit and truthfulness" (John 4:24). The word truthfulness can be translated as reality. [As mentioned in the previous chapter, *Vine's Expository Dictionary* defines truth [Greek: *aletheia*] as "the reality lying at the basis of an appearance; the manifested, veritable, essence of a matter."][3]

> The Lord also said, *"But when He, the Spirit of reality, comes, He will guide you into all the reality"* (16:13). First John 5:6 says, *"The Spirit is He who testifies, because the Spirit is the reality."* This shows us that God is Spirit, and everything related to God has to be in spirit. The Spirit of truth is the Spirit of reality. Hence, spiritual reality must be in the Holy Spirit.

> Spiritual reality is something that transcends people and things. Only that which is in the Holy Spirit is spiritual reality. All spiritual things are sustained in the Holy Spirit. Once a spiritual thing moves away from the Holy Spirit, it becomes letter and form, and it is dead. All spiritual things must be in the Holy Spirit before they can be real, living, and organic. The Holy Spirit leads us into all reality. Hence, any experience that we can acquire without the guidance of the Holy Spirit is

surely not spiritual reality. Anything that we acquire through our ears, our mind, or our emotion alone is not spiritual reality. Only the things that the Holy Spirit guides us into are spiritual reality.[4]

We do not worship God merely in the physical realm; we are to touch and tap into the spiritual reality. It is the spiritual reality of Jesus that brings life, not just the physical knowledge. Everything in the Kingdom of God is about entering into spiritual reality. It is the Spirit that brings life, and we are ministers of the Spirit.

We do not worship God merely in the physical realm;

"...God, who also made us sufficient as ministers of the new covenant, not of the letter but of the Spirit; for the letter kills, but the Spirit gives life" (2 Corinthians 3:5-6 NKJV).

The Book of Revelation shows us that John practiced this new worship in his personal life: *"I was in the Spirit on the Lord's Day..."* (Rev. 1:10). At this point, he was exiled on the island of Patmos without a church or fellowship to support him, but he still entered into the Spirit in worship. We can see from his example that we can enter into the spirit realm and worship anytime and anyplace

THE TENT OF DAVID

One of the most incredible corporate worship events in the Old Testament occurred under the leadership of three seers—Asaph, Heman, and Jeduthun. These were the same three seers who led the constant worship in David's Tabernacle for 40 years. They also each wrote psalms, which are contained in our modern Bibles (for more information, review Chapter 5, "Prophets and Seers"). At the dedication of the Temple of Solomon, as the people praised the Lord in unison, the glory of God came down as a cloud:

"...the house of the Lord, was filled with a cloud, so that the priests could not stand to minister because of the cloud; for the glory of the Lord filled the house of God" (2 Chronicles 5:13b-14 NKJV).

The focus of our attention is on the three seers who were leading when this occurred. God so enjoyed the worship that these three men created in the

Tabernacle and in the dedication service that He released His manifested presence. The Lord so loved the worship in the Tabernacle of David that it is the only Old Testament model for worship that is carried over into the New Testament.

All the animal sacrifice and all of the Old Testament altars are left behind in the New Testament in favor of what the Book of Hebrews calls a better covenant (see Heb. 8:6-13). The only exception is an obscure prophecy in Amos that says that God will raise up David's tent again:

"In that day I will restore David's fallen tent. I will repair its broken places, restore its ruins, and build it as it used to be" (Amos 9:11).

Hundreds of years later, the day finally came where the New Testament declares that God has reestablished David's tent. Peter stood before the Gentiles in Cornelius's house and, in essence, told them that God had set up a place of worship that is accessible by all people, at all times.

The words of the prophets are in agreement with this, as it is written: **"After this I will return and rebuild David's fallen tent. Its ruins I will rebuild, and I will restore it,** *that the remnant of men may seek the Lord, and all the Gentiles who bear My name, says the Lord, who does these things that have been known for ages"* (Acts 15:15-18).

One part of this restoration, which is commonly overlooked, is the restoration of seers in the worship realm. God desires to restore the constant interactive worship of David's tent. Seers need to be restored to the Body of Christ for Davidic worship to be fully restored. Prepare to hear more about worship leaders writing songs from Heaven, seeing angels during worship, and being directed by the presence of the Lord. This restoration is on the move.

ACTIVATION

Set aside this book and put on your favorite worship music. Close your eyes and engage in worship. As you do, ask the Lord to show you what is happening in the spirit realm around you. Perhaps there are spiritual beings or objects in the room with you. The next step is to ask the Lord if you should do something to engage in the spiritual experience of worship. Perhaps if you see water in the room in the spirit, the Lord might direct you to kneel down in the water and be refreshed. Step out in faith and do what the Lord directs. You can enter into an interactive experience in worship whenever you want, by faith.

ENDNOTES

1. Gary Oates, *Open my Eyes, Lord* (Dallas, GA: Open Heaven Publications, 2004), 100.

2. Ibid.

3. W.E. Vine and F.F. Bruce, *Vine's Expository Dictionary of Old and New Testament Words* (Old Tappan, NJ: Fleming H. Revell Co., 1981), 159.

4. Watchman Nee, *The Holy Spirit and Reality* (Anaheim, CA: Living Stream Ministry, 2001), 7-8.

CHAPTER 14

Entrusted with Secrets

I have wonderful news! The Lord has secrets, and He wants to entrust them to His people! He even limits His movements and activities until He has someone to share with what He is about to do. The prophet Amos said it this way: *"Surely the Lord God does nothing, unless He reveals His secret to His servants the prophets"* (Amos 3:7 NKJV).

A clear example of God revealing His secret before He would move is found in the story of Sodom and Gomorrah. The Lord spoke first to His servant Abraham about what He was going to do, and it gave Abraham the opportunity to intercede on behalf of the two cities: *"Shall I hide from Abraham what I am about to do?"* (Gen. 18:17). He desires to share with us His secrets and hear our input. There were also times that God shared His secret plan to annihilate disobedient Israel, and Moses asked God not to destroy them (Exodus 32).

When we begin to move into seeing and the prophetic, the Lord at times will begin to reveal more of His secrets to us. Remember, God does nothing unless He reveals His secret to His servants the prophets. Note that this refers specifically to His servants the prophets, not His servants the priests or His servants the kings. Those who are leaning into God to hear His voice and see into the spirit are the ones to whom He will entrust secrets.

We are under the New Covenant, where Jesus said that all of His sheep can hear His voice (see John 10:27). I am not saying that only prophets can hear the Lord and receive secrets. But the Lord takes notice of those whom He can trust with His Word. The apostle Paul goes so far as to define our identity in this way: *"...men ought to regard us as **servants of Christ** and as **those entrusted with the secret things of God**"* (1 Cor. 4:1).

Examples of the Lord Having Secrets

*"**The secret of the Lord** is with those who fear Him, and He will show them His covenant"* (Psalms 25:14 NKJV).

*"You have heard; see all this. And will you not declare it? I have made you hear new things from this time, **even hidden things,** and you did not know them"* (Isaiah 48:6).

*"At that time Jesus answered and said, 'I thank You, Father, Lord of heaven and earth, that **You have hidden these things** from the wise and prudent and have revealed them to babes. Even so, Father, for so it seemed good in Your sight'"* (Matthew 11:25-26).

*"Behold, the former things have come to pass, and new things I declare; **before they spring forth I tell you of them"*** (Isaiah 42:9 NKJV).

"But as it is written: 'Eye has not seen, nor ear heard, nor have entered into the heart of man the things which God has prepared for those who love Him.' But God has revealed them to us through His Spirit. For the Spirit searches all things, yes, the deep things of God" (1 Corinthians 2:9-10 NKJV).

*"**The secret things belong to the Lord** our God, but the things revealed belong to us and to our children forever, that we may follow all the words of this law"* (Deuteronomy 29:29).

*"It is the glory of God to **conceal a matter,** but the glory of kings is to search out a matter"* (Proverbs 25:2 NKJV).

Proper Stewardship

The secrets that the Lord shows to us each carry a weight of responsibility. Bill Johnson says, "By keeping revelation from those without hunger, God actually protects them from certain failure to carry the responsibility it would lay on them. And so He conceals."[1] Be careful what you ask for, because you have a responsibility for the revelations that the Lord shows you.

For example, when Saul had a powerful revelation of the Lord Jesus Christ on the road to Damascus, it became his responsibility to properly carry that revelation. The greater the revelation, the heavier the responsibility we have. Be careful what level of revelation you ask for, because you will be held accountable for it:

"From everyone who has been given much, much will be demanded; and from the one who has been entrusted with much, much more will be asked" (Luke 12:48b).

Later, in a similar manner Jesus said, "Whoever can be trusted with very little can also be trusted with much, and whoever is dishonest with very little will also be dishonest with much" (Luke 16:10).

Jesus also said, "Do not give dogs what is sacred; do not throw your pearls to pigs. If you do, they may trample them under their feet, and then turn and tear you to pieces" (Matthew 7:6).

If Jesus shares a secret with you, it should be treated as a pearl. Be a good steward of what He reveals. There are some people who, through ignorance or closed-minded, would not receive our sharing the secrets of God with them as a good thing. They would trample what we have shared under their feet and then turn and tear us to pieces. Jesus is warning us to use wisdom and discernment about with whom to share secrets.

Ecclesiastes 3:7 tells us that there is *a time to be silent and a time to speak.* Not every secret that the Lord shows us is intended to remain a secret forever. Perhaps there is timing for when that revelation is to be released. Many people share what God has shown them too soon, and this cuts them off from deeper revelations because they cannot be trusted.

We need to be sure that it is okay to share our information before we get ahead of God.

We need to be sure that it is okay to share our information before we get ahead of God. Ask Him if it is wise to share your revelation. If you feel any sense of hesitation in your spirit, hold back until you have a peace about sharing. This could save much criticism and broken trust from happening. There is a time to be silent and a time to speak, and some secrets are revealed over time. To reveal them early would be like having a premature baby, very dangerous and much more work than if time had been given for maturation.

I've heard Larry Randolph say, *"The true test of a prophet is not what he knows, but what he dies knowing."* There are revelations that God will entrust us with, and we will be tested on the basis of our faithfulness in keeping His secrets. Some of these things will be between us and Him for our entire life, and He will hold us accountable for these secrets. There are things that, out of relationship, I share only with my wife. These are things that only she will carry all of her life and a portion of her faithfulness can be proven by how she keeps these secrets. Our relationship to Jesus our bridegroom is similar.

Joseph

The story of Joseph is a familiar one for many. In Genesis 37, we learn that Joseph, as a young man, had two prophetic dreams from the Lord while he slept. He told his family of the dreams, and they were divided into two reactions. His father rebuked him for what was most likely arrogance, and his brothers hated him even more:

> *His brothers said to him, "Do you intend to reign over us? Will you actually rule us?" And they hated him all the more because of his dream and what he had said....When he told his father as well as his brothers, his father rebuked him and said, "What is this dream you had? Will your mother and I and your brothers actually come and bow down to the ground before you?"* **His brothers were jealous of him, but his father kept the matter in mind** (Genesis 37:8-11).

His brothers and dad responded very differently to the same revelation from God. Imagine if Joseph had not told his brothers, but had only told his father. His life may have been very different. The only difference in the story was the listener. Know your audience before you share your secrets.

Another principle from this story is that your spiritual father may be safer to share secret revelations with than those who are on your same level. Envy is often an issue between siblings (Jacob and Esau, David and his brothers, Rachel and Leah).

The Apostle John

Over the last 2,000 years, millions of people have read the Book of Revelation. In chapter 10, only the apostle John was privy to hearing what the voice of the seven thunders spoke. Jesus trusted John with this revelation and told him not to write it down for us. This was a very intimate thing for the Lord to do for John. It was private revelation meant only for John's ears.

> *"When he shouted, the voices of the seven thunders spoke. And when the seven thunders spoke, I was about to write; but I heard a voice from heaven say, 'Seal up what the seven thunders have said and do not write it down'"* (Revelation 10:3-4).

Samson's Hair

The Lord sent an angel to Samson's parents before he was born. He brought them a prophetic message about their coming child and told them that their son would be a Nazarite, which means that they were not to cut his hair, nor let him drink alcohol or touch a dead body. It is important to note that the angel never spoke of Samson's incredible strength, or the secret of his weakness. Samson's parents would be as surprised as anybody.

> *A certain man of Zorah, named Manoah, from the clan of the Danites, had a wife who was sterile and remained childless. The angel of the Lord appeared to her and said, "You are sterile and childless, but you are going to conceive and have a son. Now see to it that you drink no wine or other fermented drink and that you do not eat anything unclean, because you will conceive and give birth to a son. No razor may be used on his head, because the boy is to be a Nazarite, set apart to God from birth, and he will begin the deliverance of Israel from the hands of the Philistines* (Judges 13:2-5).

I believe that the secret of Samson's strength was a personal revelation to Samson from the Lord. At some point he came to understand the secret, keeping in mind that the angel never revealed the secret of Samson's strength. Samson's downfall would be the result of him sharing his personal revelation with Delilah:

> *"So he told her everything. 'No razor has ever been used on my head,' he said, "because I have been a Nazarite set apart to God since birth. **If my head were shaved, my strength would leave me, and I would become as weak as any other man**'"* (Judges 16:17).

I would conjecture that the power was not only in the hair on his head, but was also contained in his ability to steward the secret revelation from the Lord. When he shared the revelation, the ultimate result was that the secret was used against him.

Having put him to sleep on her lap, she called a man to shave off the seven braids of his hair, and so began to subdue him. And his strength left him (Judges 16:19).

If God entrusts private revelation to us, then we should be careful about being a good steward of His trust. If God can trust us, then He can give us power, but if we betray that trust, we *"become as weak as any other..."*

Not only did he become as weak as any other man, but the enemy took advantage of the situation, gouged out Samson's eyes, and put him into laborious bondage. This is a prophetic image of what can happen to us spiritually when we fail to steward the secrets of the Lord correctly.

King Hezekiah

King Hezekiah was extremely blessed in material goods from the Lord. He had riches, favor, silver, gold, spices, armor, gems, cattle, grain, and so on. One day, the rulers of Babylon sent out envoys to investigate what was taking place in Israel. The Word says that God left Hezekiah to test him and to know what was in his heart (see 2 Chron. 32:27-31).

*Hezekiah received the messengers and showed them **all that was in his storehouses**—the silver, the gold, the spices and the fine oil—his armory and everything found among his treasures. There was nothing in his palace or in all his kingdom that Hezekiah did not show them* (2 Kings 20:13).

King Hezekiah exercised no discretion in revealing the riches that God had given him. The handling of the riches was the test that the Lord used to prove his character. Hezekiah failed the test big time.

King Hezekiah exercised no discretion in revealing the riches that God had given him.

Then Isaiah the prophet went to King Hezekiah and asked, "What did those men say, and where did they come from?" "From a distant land," Hezekiah replied. "They came from Babylon." The prophet asked, "What did they see in your palace?" "They saw everything in my palace," Hezekiah said. "There is nothing among my treasures that I did not show them" (2 Kings 20:14-15).

As with Samson, Hezekiah received judgment for failing to steward properly. It is imperative that we learn to be good stewards who the Lord can trust. Tests will come; may we all pass through the fire unscathed.

Then Isaiah said to Hezekiah, "Hear the word of the Lord: The time will surely come when everything in your palace, and all that your fathers have stored up until this day, will be carried off to Babylon. Nothing will be left, says the LORD. And some of your descendants, your own flesh and blood that will be born to you will be taken away, and they will become eunuchs in the palace of the king of Babylon" (2 Kings 20:16-18; Isaiah 39:1-8).

SECRETS ARE A BLESSING

This chapter has had a lot of teaching about caution. I want to reemphasize that it is a blessing to receive the secrets of the Lord, and if we steward correctly, then we can enjoy the blessing without worry. Let us diligently pursue revelation from the Lord: *"But without faith it is impossible to please Him, for he who comes to God must believe that He is, and that **He is a rewarder of those who diligently seek Him"*** (Heb. 11:6).

ACTIVATION

Jesus said that the Holy Spirit will tell us of things to come (see John 16:13). Ask the Lord to show you a secret about your future. Once He has shown you something, ask Him if you can share this, with whom, and when.

Write down today's date, the guidelines the Lord gave you, and when (or if) you can share the secret.

ENDNOTES

1. Bill Johnson, *Dreaming With God* (Shippensburg, PA: Destiny Image, 2006), 60.

—Part Four—

Advanced
Seer
Training

CHAPTER 15

Seers and the End of the World

As a Seer, one of the main questions I receive is about prophetic visions and dreams regarding the end of the world. I believe that proper Biblical understanding should guide our theology, not prophetic experiences.

The main issue that I have seen is that people have divergent prophetic experiences, so how do we know which vision was correct? That is where the Bible steps in and we must test our experience. We must not believe every prophet, spirit or prophecy; they must be tested and evaluated.

"Do not treat prophecies with contempt but test them all; hold on to what is good." (1 Thessalonians 5:20-21)

"Above all, you must understand that no prophecy of Scripture came about by the prophet's own interpretation of things. For prophecy never had its origin in the human will, but prophets, though human, spoke from God as they were carried along by the Holy Spirit." (2 Peter 1:20-21)

"But even if we or an angel from heaven should preach a gospel other than the one we preached to you, let them be under God's curse!" (Galatians 1:8)

"Dear friends, do not believe every spirit, but test the spirits to see whether they are from God, because many false prophets have gone out into the world." (1 John 4:1)

In the field of endtime teachings, our movement has displayed an incredible lack of discernment and deep gullibility. For example, one Charismatic TV preacher claims that he knows his endtime teachings are right because he prays in tongues while studying. I have heard countless stories of brother so-and-so or sister-whoever that had a vision of the rapture, the antichrist or a coming great tribulation. While it is possible that they did have a vision, this does not automatically mean it was from the Lord.

Take for example the fact that much of the modern Evangelical understanding of the Rapture came about from the prophetic visions of Margaret McDonald a 15-year old girl in the 1830s. Here in her own words:

When I say, they are looking from the cross, I feel that there is much in it - they turn from the blood of the Lamb, by which we overcome, and in which our robes are washed and made white. There are low views of God's holiness, and a ceasing to condemn sin in the flesh, and a looking from him who humbled himself, and made himself of no reputation. Oh! it is needed, much needed at present, a leading back to the cross. I saw that night, and often since, that there will be an outpouring of the Spirit on the body, such as has not been, a baptism of fire, that all the dross may be put away. Oh there must and will be such an indwelling of the living God as has not been - the servants of God sealed in their foreheads - great conformity to Jesus - his holy holy image seen in his people - just the bride made comely by his comeliness put upon her. **This is what we are at present made to pray much for; that speedily we may all be made ready to meet our Lord in the air - and it will be.** Jesus wants his bride. His desire is toward us. He that shall come, will come, and will not tarry. Amen and Amen even so come Lord Jesus." (Find an online source)

Although the Rapture visions from McDonald have become the majority view in Evangelical Pop Culture, through the successes of the Scofield Reference Bible (1909) the Late Great Planet Earth (1970) and the Left Behind Series of the 1990s. In contrast there have been several books written about prophetic experiences, which present a different view of the End Times. For example the *Final Quest* series by Rick Joyner and *Visions Beyond the Veil* by H. A. Baker both seem to present a future war between Christians and evil spiritual forces. Rather than Christians avoiding a coming conflict by being raptured away, these seem to point to Christians living through the Tribulation period. Perhaps the correct interpretation of these visions is actually about our current spiritual battle in the spirit realm, but many interpretations have been applied.

One recent author has attempted to provide an interpretation of his son's prophetic experiences in *Heaven is for Real* by Todd Burpo. His four-year old son, Colton, had a near death experience in which he had many visionary experiences. In his own words:

"Dad, did you know there's going to be a war?"

"What do you mean?" Were we still on the heaven topic? I wasn't sure.

"There's going to be a war, and it's going to destroy this world. Jesus and the angels and the good people are going to fight against Satan and the monsters and the bad people. I saw it."

I thought of the battle described in the book of Revelation, and my heartbeat stepped up a notch. "How did you see that?"

"In heaven, the women and the children got to stand back and watch. So I stood back and watched." Strangely, his voice was sort of cheerful, as though he were talking about a good movie he'd seen. "But the men, they had to fight. And Dad, I watched you. You have to fight too."

(page 136)

According to Colton Burpo his father, a pastor, would still be on the earth to experience the future book of Revelation events. Yet according to Margaret McDonald's visions, all Christians would have been raptured before this. So how do we determine whose prophetic visions are correct?

This question gets even trickier when major trusted Charismatic leaders have differing views regarding the End Times. It is important that we not rally around a theological belief system simply because a lot of people respect an individual on TV, because that leader fasts a lot, or because they have had incredibly detailed visions about the future. It is our responsibility to be like the Bereans.

"Now the Berean Jews were of more noble character than those in Thessalonica, for they received the message with great eagerness and examined the Scriptures every day to see if what Paul said was true." (Acts 17:11)

Our theology must be completely founded in the Word of God.

These believers were listening to the Apostle Paul himself and yet they are commended for taking the time to research and examine his teachings in the light of Scripture. I would encourage every reader to do the same. Do not accept an End Time teaching because of who is saying it or because of their prophetic experiences. Our theology must be completely founded in the Word of God.

End Time theology falls into four basic categories:

Idealist: An Idealist believes that most of the prophetic passages in the New Testament are symbolic of the Churches struggle against darkness and we are not looking for literal fulfillment.

Historical: A Historicist believes that the prophetic passages in the New Testament have been unfolding over the course of the past 2000 years of Church history.

Futurist: A Futurist believes that most of the prophetic passages in the New Testament have not occurred and will happen in our future. (Within this system, there are divergent views regarding how the future will play out: Pre-Trib, Mid-Trib, Post-Trib, etc)

Preterist: A Preterist believes that most of the prophetic passages in the New Testament were completed by the 70AD destruction of Jerusalem.

Throughout the Church and even among Charismatics there is much disagreement and debate as to which of these is right. Although many individuals are scared of taking a strong stance or are afraid to study these topics because they seem so confusing, this is an important topic. Your understanding of the future affects how you live day-to-day in the present. The truth is that only one of the four views is correct and the other three are false, yet the debate over which one is the right one continues onward.

Although prophetic experiences sometimes confirm correct theology, the issue in this arena is that with four different categories of belief, many are willing to accept one of the four not because Scripture has convinced them but because they have been convinced by the prophetic experience of another.

For example, I recently had an individual emailing to tell me that he knew that there is a future rapture because he knows of a nine-year old boy with downs-syndrome that has seen a vision of the Rapture. Because this experience is charged with so much emotion, it is important to remember that the Word of God is the ultimate authority. Perhaps there is another downs-syndrome child that has had a vision of Christians not being raptured and living through a future tribulation. Then how would one determine which child is correct?

We must hold our visions up to the light of the Word and be willing to test them accordingly. If an End time vision is incorrect, there are several options as to why that could be:

- The devil might be bringing false experiences to create bad teaching and fear.

- The individual might be looking for more credibility or attention.

- A personal grid of theology might be slanting an individual's prophetic experiences.

It is our responsibility to test and judge, not to blindly receive everything someone is teaching.

"Above all, you must understand that no prophecy of Scripture came about by the prophet's own interpretation of things. For prophecy never had its origin in the human will, but prophets, though human, spoke from God as they were carried along by the Holy Spirit." (2 Peter 1:20-21)

All prophetic experiences must agree with the whole Word of God. As you will notice I have specifically not revealed my personal stance regarding the End Times (Endnote). It is not my goal to sway you toward my beliefs. It is my goal to sway you to study the Bible for answers. I want to encourage you *not* to take my word for it, but to test all things with the Word and hold fast that which is good.

ACTIVATION

Ask yourself the following questions:

1. Is my view of the End Times based on my personal prophetic experiences, the experiences and teachings of others or on my own responsible study of the Word?

2. Are you willing to change your understanding of the End Times if you find that the Word teaches something different?

ENDNOTE

1. (Endnote: If you are interested in reading the views of this author see, www. Raptureless.com)

CHAPTER 16

Seers and Spiritual Warfare

Because I am a seer, people often ask me about spiritual warfare. I have come to realize that I do far *less* spiritual warfare than most people do. I have an unusual perspective on warfare. I do believe that demonic forces are at work in the world, but not in the way that many think. Most true spiritual warfare takes place in the arena of *truth versus lies.* The devil is a liar, and he uses his craftiness to get us to lay aside our identity and authority. Our battle must be understood as a battle to maintain our identity, because the authority we have been given as believers is contained in our identity.

Many Christians have reached a point emotionally where they feel as though they have been stripped of their armor. They have been beaten to a pulp. They have been chained and are being dragged behind the devil's chariot as his spoils of war. Churches are filled with people that feel like Samson in the bottom of the prison. It is time that we understand what the Bible says about our identity so that we can get our authority back!

The truth regarding our identity is that we have been put into Christ. *"In Him we live and move and have our being"* (Acts 17:28). We abide in Him, and He in us (see John 15:4). We have been seated with Him in heavenly places (see Eph. 2:6). *"Greater is He who is in* [us] *than he who is in the world"* (1 John 4:4 NASB).

We should experience the truth of being *"more than conquerors"* (Rom. 8:37). Christians should be able to truly declare: *"I can do all this through Him who gives me strength"* (Phil. 4:13). The Word tells us that we are one in spirit with Him (see 1 Cor. 6:17). Therefore, the authority that we see in the life of Jesus is the authority that we have been given. He gave us the keys of the Kingdom of Heaven (see Matt. 16:19).

If we understand that we abide in Him (which also means that we abide in His authority), then our spiritual warfare is very different: we are not fighting *for* victory; we are fighting *from* victory.

We are fighting from victory.

Many have continued to fight and fight, but it is time to realize that Jesus already won the battle—and then He put us inside of Him to share this victory! Every Christian is inside of Christ, regardless of whether they are behaving perfectly or not.

*And this is the testimony: God has given us eternal life, and this life is **in His Son.** Whoever has the Son has life; whoever does not have the Son of God does not have life (1 John 5:11-12).*

With the foundation that we are in Christ and share in His authority over the devil, let's dive deeper into examining how utterly defeated the devil truly is.

The apostle Paul wrote much on the subject of spiritual warfare in the New Testament. Yet because of cultural differences, we have overlooked some of his best insights.

For example, we miss a lot of the meaning in Colossians 2:15, which says, "And having disarmed the powers and authorities, He made a public spectacle of them, triumphing over them by the cross." When Paul uses the word disarmed in this passage, he is making a first-century cultural metaphor. Paul is saying that Jesus totally stripped satan of all his power and authority. It was a term used for the disarming of a defeated foe.

The word *triumphing* is another cultural reference. When a Roman general had a notable victory, he was allowed to march his victorious armies through the streets of Rome. Behind his chariot were chained all the kings and leaders he had vanquished. They were stripped naked, chained, and pulled behind the conquering general through the streets. They were publically humiliated and openly branded as his spoils.

Paul speaks of Jesus as a conquering General enjoying a cosmic triumph (see John 12:31). In Jesus' triumphal procession are the powers of evil, beaten forever, for everyone to see. And because we have been put in Him, we are also in the chariot with Jesus.

Satan is now naked and powerless!

While many Christians feel like they are defeated warriors being dragged behind the devil's chariot, the truth is that the devil is being dragged behind their chariots! It is time for us to realize that we can maintain constant authority over the devil by remembering that we are in the chariot with Jesus! We have triumphed over satan!

We must learn to *maintain* our triumph over the devil. The Lord provided us, not only with total victory, but also with complete triumph. It is important to grasp the difference between these two words: *victory* and *triumph*. For example, at a soccer game, when the end of the game comes, the team with the most goals wins and achieves *victory*.

> ## *We must learn to* maintain *our triumph over the devil.*

Triumph is what takes place after victory has been achieved. Triumph is the celebration in the streets, the pubs, and the workplace. Triumph is the jumping up and down, the yelling and the obnoxious, grandiose boasting that occurs in the face of the losing opponent.

We are not still fighting a battle against satan, and we are not looking for victory. We are enforcing and reveling in the victory that is already ours; we are triumphing in our King Jesus. He *"...always leads us in triumph in Christ..."* (2 Cor. 2:14).

The devil wants the Church to think that we are fighting him, because he does not want the Church to understand that he has been defeated. Since his defeat was already accomplished, the Church is not on the earth to try to win a victory. Our starting point is victory, and from there we move forward. We are currently on Earth as ambassadors (see 2 Cor. 5:20; Eph. 6:19-20) enforcing and advancing the application of Jesus' victory.

> *Therefore, since the children share in flesh and blood, He Himself likewise also partook of the same, that through death* **He might render powerless** *him who had the power of death, that is,* **the devil,** *and might free those who through fear of death were subject to slavery all their lives* (Hebrews 2:14-15 NASB).

This verse is absolutely stunning, and yet it is rarely quoted in the modern spiritual warfare circles. The devil has been rendered powerless by the cross of Christ. That is an amazing truth worthy of meditation.

Another one of my favorite verses to remember about our enemy, the devil, is found in the Book of Isaiah:

> *Those who see you stare at you, they ponder your fate: "Is this the man who shook the earth and made kingdoms tremble, the man who made the world a*

wilderness, who overthrew its cities and would not let his captives go home?"
(Isaiah 14:16-17)

There will be a day when the Church looks upon satan and is shocked to see what a pitiful loser he really is. Keeping in mind that he is a total liar who accuses and deceives, what would you like to bet that he has probably talked himself up quite a bit?

If we believe what God says about us and do not buy into the lies of the devil, then we are untouchable by him.

HIS ONLY WEAPON

Remembering that we are in the chariot with Jesus and our defeated foe, satan, is being dragged behind us, we can see that the ongoing battle of spiritual warfare is simply a matter of resisting our enemy's voice. Even as he is dragged, defeated and pathetic, behind the chariot, he continues to taunt with lies, manipulations, temptation, and accusation, as well as intimidation. These are the only weapons he still has.

According to Scripture, lies are satan's stock and trade:

*Why is My language not clear to you? Because you are unable to hear what I say. You belong to your father, the devil, and you want to carry out your father's desires. He was a murderer from the beginning, not holding to the truth, for **there is no truth in him. When he lies, he speaks his native language, for he is a liar and the father of lies*** (John 8:43-44).

If we allow ourselves to listen to his voice and then come into any form of agreement with him, we are essentially stepping out of Jesus' chariot, stripping off our royal robes, and chaining ourselves beside satan.

This is the position of defeat to which many Christians have unnecessarily submitted themselves. The battle with the devil is a mind game in which he speaks to us and tries to lure us into agreement with him. One of the main mind games the devil uses is to plant thoughts or temptations in our minds. Then he tells us that these ideas are coming from the evil inside of us. This in turn causes us to condemn ourselves.

Many times I have asked Christians that are struggling with all their might against temptation if they want to sin; invariably the answer is *no.* Yet the thoughts continue to come. I would suggest that those thoughts are sourced in the voice of a demon that sounds like the old flesh nature the they used to walk in.

This explanation is likely true for many of us. That is why we must capture these thoughts and be aware of where they are coming from.

> *For though we live in the world, we do not wage war as the world does. The weapons we fight with are not the weapons of the world. On the contrary, they have divine power to demolish strongholds. We demolish arguments and every pretension that sets itself up against the knowledge of God, and* **we take captive every thought** *to make it obedient to Christ. And we will be ready to punish every act of disobedience, once your obedience is complete* (2 Corinthians 10:3-6).

We must be on guard against satan's lies. The apostle Paul said that the devil and his schemes should not outwit us, because *"...we are not unaware of his schemes"* (2 Cor. 2:11). Paul also told Timothy that demons have a theology that we Christians must be aware of. These doctrines of demons are subtle and convincing enough to lure Christians away from the faith. Paul wrote: *"The Spirit clearly says that in later times some will abandon the faith and follow deceiving spirits and things taught by demons"* (1 Tim. 4:1). Other translations use the term *doctrines of demons*.

While it is true that the devil goes about like a roaring lion, he is only able to devour those who buy into his lies. If we are aware of his schemes and do not allow him to outwit us, then we never have to end up in the lion's mouth.

> *Be alert and of sober mind. Your enemy the devil prowls around like a roaring lion looking for someone to devour. Resist him, standing firm in the faith...* (1 Peter 5:8-9).

According to the apostle John, we are literally untouchable to the devil. *"We know that anyone born of God does not continue to sin; the One who was born of God keeps them safe, and the evil one cannot harm them"* (1 John 5:18). This is the reality that comes through knowing who we are in Christ, and refusing to agree with satan's lies.

OUR WEAPONS

Since lies are what the devil uses to put people into bondage, truth is the tool that God uses to set people free. As the Bible says: *"Then you will know the truth, and the truth will set you free"* (John 8:32).

The devil is already defeated, he has already lost, and there is nothing we can do to add to what Christ accomplished on the cross.

For us to remain fixed in our triumph over the devil, we must remember two important words: *resist* and *stand*. The devil is already defeated, he has already lost, and there is nothing we can do to add to what Christ accomplished on the cross. So our current strategy is to *resist* and *stand* firm against the devil. We are standing and resisting the devil's lies, since they are the only weapons he has left.

Resist him, standing firm in the faith... (1 Peter 5:9).

...Resist the devil, and he will flee from you (James 4:7).

*Put on the full armor of God so that you can take your **stand against** the devil's schemes. ...Therefore put on the full armor of God, so that when the day of evil comes, you may be able to **stand your ground,** and after you have done everything, to **stand. Stand firm** then...* (Ephesians 6:11;13-14).

According to Ephesians 6, we have one strategy: stand against, stand our ground, stand firm. Once we understand that Jesus has already taken all of the devil's authority, we realize that our objective is not obtaining victory, but maintaining victory. Jesus obtained all authority, and then gave it to His followers. Now we are to stand and resist the devil to maintain our position of authority.

We must identify these lies and begin to stand and resist them with the truth so that we can experience the victory Christ purchased for us.

As long as we continue to believe these lies, we will remain in bondage. If we become aware of the lies that we have agreed with, we can break these agreements, step into the truth, and be set free!

ACTIVATION

I recommend carrying a notepad and pen for use with this tool. During your next week of prayer times, ask the Holy Spirit to tell you of the lies that you have believed, especially about your identity. When He shows you one of the lies, write it down. Then ask Him to tell you what the corresponding truth is regarding the lie. Begin to capture these lies and hammer them with the truths that the Holy Spirit shows you.

CHAPTER 17

Seer Orphans and Spiritual Maturity

When Karen wrote the preface to this book, we had only been traveling as conference speakers for a brief period of time. In the preface she described a group of people with the phrase I coined, *"Seer Orphans."* Since the School of the Seers became a bestseller in 2009, we have traveled extensively and met multitudes that feel like the orphans Karen described. This chapter is for them.

Although it may feel like there are dozens of different types of orphans, there is one issue that is a common thread throughout every one that I have met. The core issue for those that feel like *Seer Orphans* is an identity issue.

Whether it is the insecurity that comes from feeling misunderstood or the fear of being in relationship with church leadership because of trust issues. The majority of seers I have meet are still struggling with knowing who they are, where their value comes from and their true authority. Without these questions being answered, many issues will arise.

To see where you are at, let me ask a question. Would you be able to say "yes" to the following regarding your life?

- Is your life containing the fullness of Joy? (Psalm 16:11)
- Is your heart completely restful? (1 John 3:19-20, Mt. 11:30)
- Do you feel completely free? (2 Cor. 3:17)
- Does your life overflow with living water? (John 4:14)
- Would you describe yours as the truly abundant life? (John 10:10)

I know that this is a hard list to answer honestly, yet this is how the Bible describes the normal Christian life. If this does not describe us, then there is disconnection between the normal Christian life and us. I believe that disconnection comes from a disparity between our understanding of our identity and Jesus' view of our identity.

This is not a matter of heaping guilt. We are all constantly growing in our understanding of our identity in Christ. In fact, I believe that the main objective of our spiritual growth is understanding our identity more and more. While many have set disciplines as the mark of maturity, that is not the way of the Kingdom. Self-control is an outgrowth of the work of the Holy Spirit, not the way to force oneself to be "better" or more "mature." The more than one understands who they are, the more that self-control will naturally flow out of that identity.

THE CORE OF GROWTH

The true course of growth as a Christian is progressively understanding the fullness that we have received in Christ more and more each day. We are growing in our understanding of our position and identity in Christ. Our growth is not about achievement; Jesus already achieved everything for us. Our growth is about *receiving* the achievement that Jesus fulfilled. Many Christians try to work for a spiritual paycheck, rather than understanding that Jesus already did the work, our job is to walk in grace and to go pick up the paycheck He already earned for us. The concept that I am briefly covering in this chapter could easily fill the pages of many books, so I can do it no justice here.* Suffice it to say that this is what Paul was communicating when he wrote to the Philippians: *"Only let us live up to what we have already attained."* (Philippians 3:16) Growth is about understanding your identity. It is growth into what we already have received.

Growth is about understanding your identity.

Understanding the glorious riches of our inheritance actually requires that we receive a revelation. This does not come about simply by memorizing and quoting the Scriptures. It requires, as Paul wrote, a *"Spirit of wisdom and revelation, so that you may know"* and *"that the eyes of your heart may be enlightened in order that you may know...the riches of His glorious inheritance in His holy people."* (Ephesians 1:17-18)

GREATER LEVELS, GREATER DEVILS

One of the biggest challenges for the *Seer Orphan* is that many people gain their sense of maturity and identity from the amount of spiritual warfare they are engaged in. The clich... says "Great levels equals greater devils," therefore if one matures, then spiritual warfare increases. Also an increase in spiritual warfare is proof that one is doing something right or is important. The thinking being that the devil doesn't bother wasting his time on unimportant prey.

While these concepts are broadly accepted in Charismatic circles, I would urge you to reconsider some of them.

As I have come to understand growth in the spirit and how it intersects with spiritual warfare, I have come to a simple belief. The more identity an individual is walking in, the less that spiritual warfare is a focus. Here is an analogy to help explain my perspective.

Let's say that a man named "Steve" accepts Jesus as his Lord. After being a believer for 6 days, a demon comes along and wants to mess with Steve. At day 6 of Steve's walk with the Lord, he hasn't yet learned about his authority, identity, or his full rights as an adopted son of God.

With that in mind, add to the picture the idea that perhaps there is a scale of demons in the spirit realm ranging from 1-9, 1 being the weakest and 9 being the strongest.

At this point in Steve's spiritual walk, any demon from 1-9 can come and discourage, lie and steal from Steve.

Six month's later we come back and visit Steve again. Now he has grown in his understanding of what Jesus did for him, that Jesus gave Steve authority, that he is an ambassador of heaven, that he is a dearly beloved son. This has made it so that levels 1-4 of the demonic realm have no ability to lie to Steve because he knows better than to listen to them. They can't steal from him because he identifies them and makes them repay. Basically demons 1-4 don't even show up for a fight anymore. In this sense, Steve has moved to a greater level, therefore he is dealing with a greater level of devil. Now only demons 5-10 show up to bother him at this point.

Now six years later we visit Steve once more. He has become solid and secure in his identity, like never before. He stands on the finished work of Christ on the cross. He operates fully in sonship, He lives by faith through grace. Grace empowers and drives everything he does. For Steve, to live is Christ, to die is gain (see Phil. 1:21). At this point he is able to identify with Christ in saying that he has all authority over the devil. Steve is living as a 10. The greatest that the devil has is a 9, so Steve has become untouchable, just as John the Apostle understood himself to be.

"We know that no one who is a child of God lives in sin, but He who is God's Child keeps him, and the Evil one cannot touch him." (1 John 5:18, Weymouth)

This understanding is a challenge because many do not even believe that it is possible to live as a 10. Yet John believed it and it worked for him. Even among the apostles there were differing views. Take Paul for example, he referred to the devil as having blocked him on his travels (see 1 Thess. 2:17-18), whereas John would claim to be untouchable.

Church tradition tells us that all of the remaining 11 apostles (as well as Paul) died as martyrs, yet John did not. John had a revelation of his sonship, which kept him untouchable. John was persecuted and boiled in a vat of oil, yet it did not harm him and ultimately he had to be exiled to an island because he was truly untouchable.

If we apply my analogy to Jesus here is what we see. Jesus gets baptized in Matthew 4 and the devil (Level 9) and his cohorts (levels 1-8) are in their war room having a debate. The devil is trying to assign someone else to go tempt Jesus in the wilderness. *"Go and tempt him"* the devil barked at a level 8 demon. The demon pleaded back, *"but Jesus is the prophesied level 10, it is of no use. I am only an eight. You should go satan, you are the only level 9 here!"* So satan showed up to tempt Jesus in the wilderness, not because he ever stood a chance but because he was the highest rank and the best that the dark side had to offer. Every time that Jesus encounters demonic levels 1-8 they are in an absolute panic. They are pleading not to be thrown into the abyss, they are frightened and yelling, "We know who you are!" Demons didn't want to be there when Jesus showed up. Demons don't want to be there when you show up either, but if you don't have your identity straight, then levels 1-9 will beat on you with lies, discouragement and thievery.

It is true that as you progress in understanding your identity in Christ, you will face greater devils, if you become a level 4 in your understanding, then you will face level 5 and higher demons. But at the same time you will not be dealing with demons 1-4 because you have stepped into your authority over them. Once you move to level 7, you no longer have a struggle with levels 1-7, but you will face levels 8-9. So although you face higher levels, your overall warfare decreases because the majority of the demonic horde doesn't even want to mess around with you.

My practical recommendation is that we do not focus on warfare, but that we focus on getting a revelation of our identity in Christ. That is how we grow.

ACTIVATION

Put this prayer in your own words.

"Lord, I ask that you would give me a revelation of how you truly see me. That I would understand the heights, depths, width and length of the love you have for me. That I would fully know and experience being your child."

Take a few minutes to let Him speak to your heart. Write down what He shows you or says to you.

ENDNOTES

1. *(If you want more understanding about "identity" read *Eyes of Honor* by Jonathan Welton)

Conclusion:
From Glory to Glory

Much has already been said about how to press in by faith, walk in love, increase discernment, and so on. At this point, I want to end the book on this final note—continually push forward for more. Before you read this book, you had certain views, opinions, and understandings; hopefully, you have been stretched and challenged.

My goal has not been just to give you more information, but to create a hunger within you, to reawaken that desire to obtain more spiritual life in Jesus. We need to press in for progression, for growth, for more! I want to take this chapter to exhort you and remind you that it is the very nature of the Kingdom of God to progress. The Word says that we move:

- From grace to grace (John 1:16)
- Strength to strength (Ps. 84:7)
- Faith to faith (Rom. 1:17)
- Glory to glory (2 Cor. 3:18)
- And grow brighter and brighter (Prov. 4:18)

In Ezekiel 47:1-5, Ezekiel had a prophetic experience with the river of God. He waded into the water and took four measurements. The first measurement had the water at ankle level, the second at the knees, the third up to the waist, and the final measurement had the water over his head. This is a clear picture of the nature of the

Kingdom of God; we should be progressing until we are in way over our heads in the river of God.

One of the messianic prophecies over Jesus was, *"Of the increase of His government and peace there shall be no end..."* (Isa. 9:7). Jesus set in motion a Kingdom that is still progressing and being established more and more each day.

Jesus said it this way: *"The Kingdom of Heaven is like a mustard seed planted in a field. It is the smallest of all seeds, but it becomes the largest of garden plants; it grows into a tree, and birds come and make nests in its branches"* (see Matt. 13:31-32).

Jesus also used this illustration:

The Kingdom of Heaven is like the yeast a woman used in making bread. Even though she put only a little yeast in three measures of flour, it permeated every part of the dough (see Matt. 13: 33).

The Kingdom of God is never stagnant; it is always progressing forward and taking ground.

THE NATURE OF GOD'S RELATIONSHIP WITH US

Sometimes we in the Church have said that if God wants us to grow, then He will just do all the work. I hope that nobody consciously thinks this, but it is declared loud and clear by the actions and lifestyle of many. This lazy approach to the Christian walk is connected to an extremely inaccurate view of the sovereignty of God. We find a great example of God Himself correcting this view in the story of Moses.

*Moses answered the people, "Do not be afraid. Stand firm and you will see the deliverance the Lord will bring you today. The Egyptians you see today you will never see again. **The Lord will fight** for you; **you need only to be still.**" Then the Lord said to Moses, "Why are you crying out to me? Tell the Israelites to **move on**. Raise your staff and stretch out your hand over the sea to divide the water so that the Israelites can go through the sea on dry ground* (Exodus 14:13-16).

Our understanding of the sovereignty of God will determine whether we continue to progress with God. He reigns over all, but He has given us authority that He wants us to operate in so we can move forward in our call and destiny. If we sit by and just say that God will handle everything, then we don't understand the nature of God's relationship with us, and we will not move forward with the Lord. The Word says that He has given us everything we need for life and godliness and that we are to walk out our salvation with fear and trembling. We need to hunger and thirst for righteousness, to press in for more, to pursue love and the spiritual gifts. I believe that we are especially living in a time where we are called to pursue the gift of Discerning of Spirits. This gift needs to be restored to the Body of Christ.

RESTORING DISCERNING OF SPIRITS

I recently was reading through a "spiritual gifts for dummies" type of book. As I looked at the table of contents, I noticed that there was a chapter listed for each of the nine gifts. Discerning of spirits and prophecy had been grouped together in one chapter. I flipped through the 20 pages of this combined chapter and found that the first 18 pages were about prophecy only, and the last 2 pages were about discerning of spirits. In this 165-page foundational book, there were only 2 pages on this neglected gift of the Spirit. Within the two pages there were at least five noncommittal statements about what this gift "might be," "could possibly be," or "perhaps could be." The author wasn't even sure what this gifting is.

Then I did a search online for discernment ministries. The top ten results on a Google search yielded the most antiÐHoly Spirit, judgmental and harsh Web sites. Filled with hatred and bearing false witness, these sites offer a discernment that originates from the flesh and not the supernatural gift of the Holy Spirit. I say all this to reinforce that discerning of spirits desperately needs to be restored to the modern Church.

Of the nine gifts of the Holy Spirit, eight of the gifts have each gone through a process of being restored (Acts 3:21) into a place of prominence in the Church. Let me explain.

The gifts of tongues and interpretation of tongues both went through a process of being restored to the Church starting in 1906 at the Azusa Street Revival. Since then, these two gifts have gained normalcy in many denominations. The gifts of healing and word of knowledge were restored to the Church through the 1948 Voice of Healing movement. After this, the gift of faith was brought back to the Church by such wonderful teachers as Kenneth Hagin, Kenneth Copeland, and the Word of Faith movement. The gifts of prophecy and word of wisdom were brought back by the ministry of Christian International, the Kansas City Prophets, and the Vineyard movement in the 1980s.

The only two gifts that have not yet been through a full restoration are the gift of miracles and the gift of discerning of spirits. I believe that the gift of miracles has started to be restored as of the mid-1990s. Consider the vast miracles that have happened under such ministers as Heidi Baker, David Hogan, Bill Johnson, Randy Clark, and many others. There have been thousands upon thousands of miraculous physical healings taking place around the world. Also, there have been hundreds of people raised from the dead in the last 15 years. I believe that we are currently experiencing the restoration of the gift of miracles to the Body of Christ. Consider the unexplainable manifestations of God's glory, such as gold dust, heavenly manna, heavenly gemstones, feathers falling in meetings, limbs growing out, instantaneous weight-loss, and others.

Forerunners

Every gift that has gone through restoration has had a group of people working to restore the gift. Whether prophets, apostles, healers, teachers, or evangelists, God always raises up forerunners before He initiates the restoration. Currently, He has set in the Church those with the spiritual gifting as seers to train others in the gift of discerning of spirits. In this next move of the Holy Spirit, because it is their primary gifting, God will be using seers to teach the rest of the Body of Christ how to operate in the gift of discerning of spirits. Prepare to hear more about seers in the years ahead.

Why Is Discernment Last?

I believe that the gift of discerning of spirits is purposefully the last gift on God's agenda for restoration to the Church. Let me lay a foundation for why I would make such a statement.

First, we know that we are looking forward to a day where the Church will come to the *"unity of the faith"* (Eph. 4:11-13). A day will come when the Church has risen in unity and glory to the full stature of Jesus Christ.

Second, Jesus prayed that we (the Church) would be one as He and the Father are one (see John 17:21). I believe Jesus' prayer will be answered. The Church will walk in the same unity that Jesus and the Father walked in.

Third, and most importantly, for true unity to be restored to the last day's Church, there has to be a restoration of the love of God in the Body of Christ.

These verses point to a day of unity and love in the Church like we have not yet seen. Remember that one definition I gave of discerning of spirits is, "Seeing the situations and people around you as if you were looking through the eyes of Jesus." We need to have this gift restored for us to see others properly through pure eyes of Jesus' love. True love among brothers must be restored before true unity will manifest. Not only do we need to have this gift in place for that day to come, but it is also the last of the nine gifts that still needs restoration.

LOVE AND DISCERNMENT

As we learned in this book, discerning of spirits is always hand in hand with love. I believe that the restoration of discerning of spirits is the final bridge to the movement of love and unity in the Church.

And this I pray, that your **love** *may abound still more and more in knowledge and all* **discernment** (Philippians 1:9 NKJV).

The revelation is this: "When the Body of Christ sees thro the eyes of love (discernment), then we will be walking in true love and unity." Love and discernment are irrevocably linked.

Here is the spiritual progression to be looking for in the next few decades:

1. Seers are being set in the Church by God.

2. Seers are going to teach and train the Church about discerning of spirits.

3. The Church will then begin to see each other through the eyes of Jesus.

4. This will bring about an unprecedented movement of God-like love.

5. True God-like love will bring about a move of true God-like unity.

6. The *"unity of the faith"* (Eph 4:11-13) will be fulfilled, and *"we* [the Church will] *be one as He and the Father are one"* (John 17:21) will also be fulfilled.

7. This completes one of the final prophecies that must be fulfilled before Jesus can bring about the New Heaven and New Earth (see Rev. 22).

A WORD FROM THE LORD

I am going to conclude with a declaration I believe is from the Lord about the next move of the Holy Spirit:

The gift of discerning of spirits will be the next gifting restored to the Church. As the Lord's people see each other through the eyes of Jesus, a great unity will come forth. The breaking down of denominational divisions and walls will continue with great increase. Brothers and sisters throughout the Church will come together as one body like never before. Then the Lord's heart of love will be fully expressed through His Bride, His people, His Church.[1]

ACTIVATION

Make a plan for integrating godly habits for growth. Start with what you have learned here and then expand upon it. This is only the beginning.

Enter worship in Spirit and in Truth.

Regularly behold Jesus.

Pursue impartation.

Keep your spiritual eyes clean.

Write a letter to yourself from Jesus.

Acknowledge the love shed abroad in your heart.

Ask the Lord to share secrets with you.

PRACTICE THE FOUR KEYS:

1. Fasting and prayer
2. Praying in the Spirit
3. Hearing from God
4. Fellowshiping with people of faith

DECLARE TO THE LORD:

1. *Jesus, I will pursue you no matter what.*

2. *I will overcome offense and disappointment to follow You.*

3. *I will follow, full of faith.*

FIVE MEDITATIONS

1. Good Things

2. The Word of God

3. Prophetic Words

4. The Lord Himself

5. The Works of God

ENDNOTES

1. Jonathan Welton, October 20, 2008.

—INTERACTIVE—
STUDY GUIDE

How to Use This Interactive Study Guide

This Expanded Edition of School of the Seers includes the following study guide to help you grow and apply the knowledge you've gained through the readings and activation exercises. We encourage you to gather a small group of like-minded friends and take the time to work through this guide. Have your Bible, a pen, and a journal, together with this book. Read the chapters; take the time to DO the activation exercises and journal your experiences. Work through the study guide questions that follow and come together with your group prepared to encourage each other! Hold one another accountable in the memory work, too!

As you prepare to use this study, you can go to the following website to see videos of Jonathan teaching on the very topics you are studying. Go to:

www.Jonwelton.com/SOTS

Introduction

Teaching Points

- Laying a biblical foundation for the Body of Christ to experience what the "no-name" servant experienced.

- Supernatural counterfeits

- Book Overview

Key Scriptures

(in order of appearance in chapter)

1 Kings 19:19-21

2 Kings 2:12-14

2 Kings 4:12a

2 Kings 5:20-27

2 Kings 6:15-17

Flip the Switch

An ever-increasing and consistent relationship with the Lord is much more important than an experience, and I want to caution you not to employ or tackle this teaching unless your life demonstrates intense passion, desire, and yearning for God, His righteousness and His presence. Moreover, that your life demonstrates First Corinthians 13:2 in which Paul states, "...without love, we are nothing." Further in this teaching you will learn that we must *activate* our faith. Faith works through love, God being love. If you are walking in an intimate and personal relationship with God, you will hear and see what the Father is doing, and will join Him in His work.

S-T-R-E-T-C-H

Please read the following six verses,—can you relate?

[The prophet Jeremiah] *"When your words came, I ate them; they were my joy and my heart's delight, for I bear your name, O Lord God Almighty"* (Jeremiah 15:16).

[Psalm of David] *When he was in the Desert of Judah]* *"O God, You are my God, earnestly I see You; my soul thirsts for You, my body longs for You, in a dry and weary land where there is no water" (Psalm 63:1).*

[Mark concerning Jesus] *"Very early in the morning, while it was still dark, Jesus got up, left the house and went off to a solitary place, where He prayed"* (Mark 1:35)

[Paul to the Philippians] *What is more, I consider everything a loss compared to the surpassing greatness of knowing Christ Jesus my Lord, for whose sake I have lost all things. I consider them rubbish, that I may gain Christ"* (Philippians 3:8-10).

"Neither do men pour new wine into old wineskins. If they do, the skins will burst, the wine will run out and the wineskins will be ruined. No, they pour new wine into new wineskins, and both are preserved" (Matthew 9:17).

"My soul yearns for You in the night; in the morning my spirit longs for You. When Your judgments come upon the earth, the people of the world learn righteousness." (Isaiah 26:9a).

REVIEW

1. We are supernatural beings having a _____ physical experience.

2. Where is the spirit realm?

3. What is a seer orphan?

4. Satan operates his kingdom by _____ the true Kingdom of God.

JOURNAL

Write a specific resolve for strengthening your relationship with God. In what areas can you improve the quality of your spiritual health?

PONDER & MEMORIZE

"Come near to God and He will come near to you" (James 4:8a)

"Then Jesus declared, "I am the Bread of life. He who comes to Me will never go hungry, and he who believes in Me will never be thirsty" (John 6:35).

CHAPTER ONE

The Mantle of Fire and Water

TEACHING POINTS

- We must take responsibility for this function
- Most of the time we activate/switch this on by acts of faith
- We cooperate with the Holy Spirit

KEY CHAPTER SCRIPTURES

(in order of appearance in chapter)

John 5:8

Mark 2:9

John 9:11

Luke 17:11-19

Deuteronomy 4:11

Psalm 18:11-12

Psalm 97:2-4

Psalm 133

FLIP THE SWITCH

We must learn to take responsibility for the function of seeing in the spirit, and develop our use of it to minister to the Body *as directed/led by the Holy Spirit.* Take time to seek and fine-tune yourself to be led by the Spirit of God. Ask yourself, is the direction I am taking consistent with the Word of God? The Holy Spirit never directs us contrary to His Word, which is why you must hide His Word in your heart. His Word will give you clarity and a good sense of whether you are being directed/led by the Spirit.

How might the Holy Spirit lead you for the healing of a person? Provide an example, and test/confirm by way of a verse or passage in the Word. How then, would you activate your faith...flip on the switch, for the miracle?

_____

_____

_____

_____

_____

_____

_____

_____

_____

_____

S-T-R-E-T-C-H

Please read the following verses. Which are sovereign acts of God, and which ones require flipping a switch?

1. *"All these are the work of one and the same Spirit, and He gives them to each one, just as He determines"* (1 Corinthians 12:11).

2. *"Then Jesus said to him, 'Get up! Pick up your mat and walk.'"* (John 5:8).

3. *"My sheep listen to My voice; I know them, and they follow Me. I give them eternal life, and they shall never perish; no one can snatch them out of My hand"* (John 10:27-28).

4. *"Which is easier: to say to the paralytic, 'Your sins are forgiven,' or to say, 'Get up, take your mat and walk?'"* (Mark 2:9).

5. *"He replied, 'The man they call Jesus made some mud and put it on my eyes. He told me to go to Siloam and wash. So I went and washed, and then I could see.'"* (John 9:11).

6. *"The Lord opened her heart to respond to Paul's message"* (Acts 16:14b).

The seer realm is thrilling because it is God communicating/revealing to us in the present, through a process of visualization, right here, right now, giving us additional opportunity to know and see into His heart and mind those things that move and touch Him, and it helps us to be in step with what God is doing here on earth today! Are you ready to be s-t-r-e-t-c-h-e-d beyond natural limits? Open your eyes! When you open your eyes there is no limit to how far you can see in the spirit. His dreams for you are greater than your greatest dreams. Your faith to believe God will be stretched, as you learn to rely on His goodness and His grace.

REVIEW

1. In order to step into the things of the Kingdom realm: healing, prophecy, miracles, discerning of spirits, what usually has to happen?

2. What is a mantle?

3. True or false: Visions can be switched on and off.

4. True or false: Each of our experiences can differ from one to another.

5. True or false: As we start out as newbies seeing in the spirit, we should not shout out everything we see; not until we've had practice/experience.

JOURNAL

As you learn to walk in the seer realm, remember, it is like climbing UP a ladder, from the lowest rung, and up, up, up, step by step; it is something you'll grow in, and, if you keep at it, keep flipping the switch, and commit to it, you'll develop your seer ability. The key is, stay close to the Lord at whatever rung you are on, remain obedient, and move *with Him,* always seeking to edify people in a way that glorifies God!

A good part of your "training" is to learn how to differentiate what you see as of the Spirit of God. It helps to record your experiences and reflections and learning curves in a separate journal, which over time will become a valuable reference to you, helping you fine-tune things as you grow.

Ponder & Memorize

"I pray also that the eyes of your heart may be enlightened in order that you may know the hope to which He has called you, the riches of His glorious inheritance in the saints, and his incomparably great power for us who believe. That power is like the working of His mighty strength, which He exerted in Christ when He raised Him from the dead and seated Him at His right hand in the heavenly realms" (Ephesians 1:18-20).

I will live and operate out of the brightness of HIS presence!

CHAPTER TWO

Spiritual Senses

TEACHING POINTS

1. Seeing in the spirit: function of the true gift of discerning of spirits

2. The gift of discernment communicates/functions through our spiritual senses

3. Three sets of five senses

4. Spiritual sight=eyes of the heart

5. Spiritual senses similar to the physical though largely under-developed

6. Soul Senses, Spirit Senses, Physical Senses

KEY CHAPTER SCRIPTURES

(in order of appearance in chapter)

1 Corinthians 12

1 Thessalonians 5:23

2 Kings 6:17

Ephesians 1:8

Ezekiel 3:1-3

2 Corinthians 2:14

Luke 8:43-46

Matthew 5:8

Flip the Switch

Before you became a Christian, did you ever try to read the Bible, and fail to really grasp the message of the Gospel? The prophecies of the Old Testament? Did you lack revelation and understanding for what you read? How it changes after we become believers in Christ Jesus, our spiritual eyes open and suddenly the Bible has so much more depth and meaning and purpose! Suddenly we even *see* Christ in the Old Testament. And most new believers, are singularly focused on God in the beginning, especially. Sadly, sometimes we lose that blush of new love, and the revelations that accompany it, why? Because we lose our focus. So you *do* have spiritual eye-opening experience! And spiritual eyes. They just needed to be opened. And kept open!

The key to begin to see, and to keep our eyes opened and seeing, is found in Matthew 5:8: "Blessed are the pure in heart for they shall *see* God." "Pure" meaning, our hearts have to be focused whole-heartedly, on God. To focus wholeheartedly, we must remove distractions: clutter, the dross of life.

- What is distracting you from focusing on God?
- And how can you go about re-aligning your focus?
- How will you deal with the distractions?

S-T-R-E-T-C-H

Please read the following excerpt from Paul's letter to the Ephesians. What life changing truths does God want you/us to see? And do you, have you "seen" these things? If your heart is not yet enlightened, focus on God!

"For this reason, ever since I heard about your faith in the Lord Jesus and your love for all the saints, I have not stopped giving thanks for you, remembering you in my prayers. I keep asking that the God of our Lord Jesus Christ, the glorious Father, may give you the Spirit of wisdom and revelation, so that you may know Him better. I pray also that the eyes of your heart may be enlightened in order that you may know the hope to which he has called you, the riches of his glorious inheritance in the saints, and His incomparably great power for us who believe. That power is like the working of His mighty strength, which He exerted in Christ when He raised him from the dead and seated Him at His right hand in the heavenly realms, far above all rule and authority, power

and dominion, and every title that can be given, not only in the present age but also in the one to come. And God placed all things under His feet and appointed Him to be head over everything for the church, which is His body, the fullness of Him who fills everything in every way" (Ephesians 1:15-23).

Life Changing Truths:

1. _____
_____
_____
_____
_____

2. _____
_____
_____
_____
_____

3. _____
_____
_____
_____
_____

4. _____
_____
_____
_____
_____

Review

1. Jesus was speaking in Matthew 5:8 of purity as a key to _____.

2. What is the meaning of pure as it relates to that verse? _____.

3. To be able to focus on God we have to remove _____.

4. What are the five spiritual senses?

    1. _____

    2. _____

    3. _____

    4. _____

    5. _____

5. Every person also has five senses in their _____ and five _____ senses.

6. The condition of our soul affects the way we _____ the world, the way we _____ others, our willingness to _____ certain things, or how we react to _____ certain things.

7. The physical senses interact with the _____ realm, the soul senses interact with the _____ realm; and the spirit has senses that interact with the _____ realm.

Journal

Record the following: the most beautiful sight you have ever seen? The loveliest fragrance you have ever smelled? The most pleasurable thing you have ever touched? The most precious sound you have ever heard? A most memorable taste? Did those experiences evoke emotions? Reactions? Did they change you in some way?

What is the ugliest/most disturbing, putrid thing you've ever laid eyes on? The grossest odor you've ever smelled? The slimiest dirtiest thing you've ever touched? The scariest sound you've ever heard? The most foul thing you've ever tasted? Record your reactions. How did these experiences make you feel?

As you record your thoughts and reactions concerning these events, keep in mind, that the events that you experience now and in the future through your spiritual senses may evoke similar responses, because they operate in much the same way.

PONDER & MEMORIZE

"But thanks be to God, who always leads us in triumphal procession in Christ and through us spreads everywhere the fragrance of the knowledge of Him" (2 Corinthians 2:14).

I will NOT lose my focus!

CHAPTER THREE

Impartation

TEACHING POINTS

- Biblical truths and facts relating to impartation
- Impartation is foundational, intentional, biblical, individual, a seed,
- Relationship to the anointing
- You can only impart what you possess

KEY CHAPTER SCRIPTURES

(in order of appearance in chapter)

1 John 2:27

Hebrews 6:1-2

Romans 1:11

Acts 3:6

Deuteronomy 34:9

Numbers 24-25a

2 Kings 2:9

1 Timothy 4:14

Luke 8:4-15

John 7:38-39

2 Corinthians 4:4

2 Kings 2:10

1 Timothy 5:22

1 Timothy 3

1 Timothy 5:17-20

Flip the Switch

The more revelation we receive, the greater our burden of responsibility. Spiritual hunger *prepares our heart* to carry the weight, our character upholds it. If we are not walking in a mature stature in Christ Jesus, we cannot possibly safely steward the power, thus, become a danger to those around us. Consequently, not everyone receives the same level of impartation; not everyone receives equal portions, certainly, never more than one can carry or handle. God may even remove an an anointing for a season if necessary.

Evaluate your character. If you are not in a good place: secret sin, compromise, double standards, unforgiveness, excessive unrelated busyness, pride; if you are fearful, timid, unmindful, critical, you need to do some housecleaning.

S-T-R-E-T-C-H

Review again the Parable of the Sower found in Luke 8:4-15. This seed principle is also true of how we receive from God. If you are imparted to, the seed you've received will grow in proportion to the quality of the soil in which it is planted, and in the maintenance and care of the soil. The richer and more nutritious the soil, the quicker, healthier, and stronger it will grow. How well watered are you? *How much of the SON's light are you experiencing every day?*

Hint: Train your spiritual perception/sight through constant use of the Word of God; this will give your spiritual senses the ability to quickly and accurately discern what is of God and what is not, and help your mind, will, and emotions, to process what you're seeing or hearing.

Review
True or False

1. Impartation is important to helping you get established.

2. The laying on of hands (Hebrews 6:1-2) is not a fundamental doctrine.

3. Impartation always happens by accident.

4. A transferring anointing or impartation can be stirred up by the laying on of hands.

5. Any believer can declare and impart a gift or anointing upon another by the laying on of hands.

6. Impartation was only introduced in the New Testament.

7. The Holy Spirit leads someone to lay hands on a person intentionally to impart something.

8. Oil is symbolic of the anointing.

9. You cannot impart a double portion if you only have a single portion.

JOURNAL

The woman who touched Jesus' garment intentionally pulled on the healing anointing that He had. Prepare the soil for what you need. Pull on Jesus for something He has, then record His response.

PONDER / MEMORIZE

"Then the Lord opened Balaam's eyes, and he saw the Angel of the Lord standing in the road with His sword drawn. So he bowed low and fell face-down" (Numbers 22:31).

I'm contending for a DOUBLE portion!

CHAPTER FOUR

We Can All See

TEACHING POINTS

- Spiritual gifts can be taught, learned, activated
- All nine gifts reside in us
- Three levels of gifts
- Faith level of operation
- God's desire is for every believer to operate in spiritual sight
- Eagerly desire and pursue the greater gifts

KEY CHAPTER SCRIPTURES

(in order of appearance in chapter)

1 Corinthians 12:1

1 Corinthians 14:31

2 Timothy 1:6

Hebrews 5:14

1 Corinthians 12:7-11

1 Peter 4:10

Mark 16:17, 18

Matthew 10:8

Ephesians 4:11-13

1 Corinthians 12:10

Mark 8:18

Hebrews 5:12-14

Ephesians 1:15-18

2 Kings 6:15-17

Revelation 3:17-18

Luke 4:18

Matthew 7:1-5

1 John 2:9-11

1 Corinthians 12:31

Flip the Switch

The ability to discern is an ability from God to every believer. The anointing to see (Revelation 3:17-18) is a provision God has made available to you. He has also given you an anointing to heal the sick, cleanse the leper, prophesy. Freely we received, freely we give. We can employ these "all can" faith gifts in our walks. You can and should have your spiritual eyes and ears open and functioning.

S-T-R-E-T-C-H

Hate and unforgiveness can blind your spiritual eyes. It will hinder, obscure, destroy, and obstruct Christ-like discernment. Determine today to operate your discernment only in unconditional love.

Review

True or False

1. Because you have the ability to discern, you have the gift of discerning of spirits, and therefore are in the office and calling of a seer.

2. Paul believed that all Christians could have their spiritual eyes opened.

3. If I don't have a gift of healing, I am not responsible for praying for the sick.

4. God asks that we all discern good from evil.

JOURNAL

Over the next while, record your dreams as soon as you awaken in the morning. Provide details: colors, shapes, words, anything you remember seeing or hearing, even smelling in your dream. How did you feel seeing what you saw? Ask God to help you discern the meaning of your dream.

PONDER/MEMORIZE

"Anyone who lives on milk, being still an infant, is not acquainted with the teaching about righteousness. But solid food is for the mature, who by constant use have trained themselves to distinguish good from evil" (Hebrews 5:13, 14).

I eagerly DESIRE the GREATER gifts!

CHAPTER FIVE

Prophets and Seers

Teaching Points

- Defining seers and prophets, their functions
- Distinguish Seers and Prophets
- Seers of the Bible

Key Chapter Scriptures

(in order of appearance in chapter)

1 Chronicles 29:29

2 Samuel 15:27

2 Chronicles 16:7

2 Chronicles 9:29

Amos 7:12

2 Chronicles 29:30

2 Chronicles 35:15

1 Chronicles 25:5

1 Samuel 9:9

Ephesians 4:11

2 Kings 6:17

Flip the Switch

You, as a Christian have legal access to see into the spirit realm around you, an unbeliever, without Christ, does not. As you grow in the seer anointing, God will communicate with you more from visions and dreams than audible words. Your experiences will be more visual, revelation from the Lord taught to you as dreams, mental pictures, visions, such as open visions, via angelic messengers, or experiences in Heaven. God may give you revelation in only one visual manner, or a variety, or, He may give you the ability to use your eyes to see as Elisha did, where he saw the hills full of horses and chariots of fire all around Elisha. So, declare right now: I have legal access to see into the spirit realm.

S-T-R-E-T-C-H

If you or a loved one are in a hard situation, pray: Lord, open my eyes so I may see, as Elisha did.

REVIEW
TRUE OR FALSE

1. A seer will often say, "The Lord showed me..."

2. Prophets in the Old Testament at one time were called "seers."

3. The seer anointing cannot be passed generationally.

4. God communicates with seers and prophets so they can communicate His messages and declare them to the Church to bring vision, direction, and encouragement.

JOURNAL

Over the next while, record the various ways in which the Holy Spirit communicates messages to you. Do you see a pattern emerging?

PONDER/MEMORIZE

"Love never fails. But where there are prophecies, they will cease; where there are tongues, they will be stilled; where there is knowledge, it will pass away. For we know in part and we prophesy in part, but when perfection comes, the imperfect disappears" (1 Corinthians 13:8-10).

I see hills FULL of horses and chariots of fire!

The Unseen Realm

TEACHING POINTS

- Defining the realms & terms
- Spiritual dynamics/natural consequences
- Seeing into the realms

CHAPTER SCRIPTURES

(in order of appearance in chapter)

2 Corinthians 4:18

Genesis 1

Revelation 22

Daniel 10:13

2 Corinthians 12:2-4

2 Kings 6:13-17

Daniel 10:4-7

Daniel 10:8-11

Revelation 1:9-18

Numbers 22:21-27; 28-23

FLIP THE SWITCH

Daniel lived a life full of incredible spiritual experiences. As did the Apostle John, Stephen, and many others. And you can too, even in the midst of the greatest hardships. Sometimes this is when we become most open to messages from the Lord, when our eyesight is at its sharpest. If you are going through trials, are burnt out, persecuted, God can work with that! *Be open to what He wants to show you.*

Through the supernatural enabling of the Holy Spirit, you will be able to see spiritual realities, perhaps even the heavens open, and the Son of Man standing at the right hand of God, as Stephen did, while being stoned for his testimony.

S-T-R-E-T-C-H

Many Bible characters experienced and interacted with the unseen realm. Even as angels worked with the saints of old, they will work with us today. You have access, and should experience this realm in your life too. Angels are all around us, and you will see them if you have eyes to see them. Remember to open your eyes!

REVIEW

1. True or False? The "seen" realm is also called the "physical" realm, which we can experience through our natural five senses.

2. The physical realm and spiritual realm, Paul referred to as _____ and_____.

3. The eternal realm is any realm other than the _____ realm.

4. The_____ realm is the physical realm.

5. True or False: The spirit realm is far more real than the physical realm.

6. Angels came come to earth from Heaven, but they can also surround us on the earth in the_____ realm.

7. True or False: Elisha saw into the unseen realm of the spirit.

8. The unseen realm is only good.

JOURNAL

Write your thoughts concerning this statement: You are one heartbeat away from existing entirely in the spirit realm.

PONDER/MEMORIZE

"He reveals deep and hidden things; He knows what lies in darkness, and light dwells with Him" (Daniel 2:22).

I want to SEE from Heaven's PERSPECTIVE!

CHAPTER SEVEN

Questions
About the Angelic Realm

No Study Necessary

Discerning of Spirits

TEACHING POINTS

- Natural and supernatural discernment
- The human spirit
- Four different areas of supernatural discernment
- Judgment and discernment
- Four types of spirits
- Five Filters

KEY CHAPTER SCRIPTURES

(in order of appearance in chapter)

1 Corinthians 12

1 Corinthians 2:14

1 Thessalonians 5:21

Luke 12:56

Matthew 7:1, 2

John 7:24

Acts 2, Acts 8

John 1:32-34

2 Kings 6

Numbers 22

Ephesians 6:16; 17

Proverbs 12:18

Isaiah 54:17

2 Corinthians 7:1

Hebrews 4:12

Luke 13:11-13

Galatians 6:1, 2

John 4:16-19

2 Peter 1:19

Psalm 12:6

Matthew 7:15, 16

Galatians 5:22, 23

1 John 2:20; 26-27

Ephesians 4:11-13

Colossians 3:15

Psalm 103:2-7

Flip the Switch

The gift of discerning of spirits is a supernatural gift from the Holy Spirit to be operated through love. Never is it to operate as a vehicle to condemn, criticize, suspect, manipulate, or accuse. Check your motivation, if you are gossiping, back-biting, dishonoring, or smearing anyone, stop and repent! God may also just hold the gift back for a season, until you do.

S-T-R-E-T-C-H

Try to view people through the eyes of Jesus. In so doing, you can't be carrying a record of wrongs or suspicions. Forgive the record, and repent for having held it. This way you will be able to rely on clear discernment. What to do if you pick up something negative? Pray on the person's behalf, or, bring him or her into healing, just as Jesus did in His encounter with the Samaritan woman.

REVIEW

1. True or False: The biblical words judgment and discernment are sometimes used synonymously.

2. The Greek root words for judgment (anakrino, dokimazo) give us two base meanings that are good to provide insight into the nature of discernment; they are _____, _____.

3. List the four types of spirits we can discern:

   1. _____

   2. _____

   3. _____

   4. _____

4. Who at Pentecost discerned the Holy Spirit?

5. What is the best course of action to take when you discern something outside your comfort zone?

6. What is a heavenly spirit?

7. True or False: The discerning of a human spirit can bring emotional, physical, and spiritual healing to someone.

8. The human soul is not inherently evil or it would not have existed in _____.

9. The flesh is the _____ nature of the spirit, soul, or body.

10. True or False: When we in the spirit realm discern the human spirit/soul, we may acquire only bad information.

11. Discerning of spirits is a supernatural gift from the Holy Spirit to be operated through_____.

12. True or false: Not everyone around you may "see" what you see.

JOURNAL

Write your thoughts concerning this statement: "In the spirit, words equal swords, so with our mouths we also wield swords. Now consider: Who in your life is experiencing sickness of the heart, and what words and actions can you use/take to remove the spiritual arrows that afflict them? What filters should you employ in your discernment to determine the good and the bad?

Ponder/Memorize

"Stop judging by mere appearances, and make a right judgment" (John 7:24).

The BIBLE is my BASIS for Understanding God's Nature

CHAPTER NINE

Hindrances to Discernment

TEACHING POINTS

- Spiritual violations
- Maintaining clarity

KEY CHAPTER SCRIPTURES

(in order of appearance in chapter)

Luke 9:54-56

Philippians 4:6

Proverbs 29:25

Job 1:9-10

1 Peter 5:7

Matthew 13:12

Mark 8:33

Luke 9:52

Acts 8:18-24

2 Kings 17:35-38

Matthew 5:27-28

Matthew 6:22-23

Psalm 101:3

Flip the Switch

Re-read the above key scriptures, really take your time to ponder and deeply root these truths in your heart to help "mature" and develop your spirit in the Lord and in His truths.

S-T-R-E-T-C-H

Identify: What do you see as a "weakness" in your life, a limitation that has hindered your spiritual growth? Fear of conflict? Lack of energy? Double minded-ness? A habit? Unforgiveness? Stress? Lust? Now ask God to identify what He sees as hindrances? Do His thoughts and yours, agree?

Review

1. We have to be careful of the _____ that we feed our _____.

2. How can what we watch on television, or even over the Internet, negatively influence our ability to discern accurately?

3. Before you watch a program, what should you do?

4. What is the best remedy for removing emotional wounds?

5. True or false: A heart of peace will sharpen our visual acuity.

6. A heart of fear will _____ you in.

Journal

Why do you wish to develop your "seeing" gift? And how will it glorify God and benefit others? How does it benefit you? Are your motives pure? Be honest.

Ponder/Memorize

"Everyone who competes in the games goes into strict training. They do it to get a crown that will not last; but we do it to get a crown that will last forever" (1 Corinthians 9:25).

Hedge me in LORD!

CHAPTER TEN

The Force of Love

TEACHING POINTS

- Looking through the eyes of Jesus
- Definition of love
- Walking/operating in love
- Increasing the love force

KEY CHAPTER SCRIPTURES

(in order of appearance in chapter)

First Corinthians 12, 13, 14

1 Thessalonians 5:8

1 Timothy 6:11

2 Timothy 2:22

1 John 1:6b

Ephesians 5:2

Jude 1:21

1 Peter 4:8

Colossians 3:12, 14

Ephesians 3:17b-19

Colossians 1:19

John 3:16

Romans 5:6-8

1 John 3:14

1 John 4:16-17

John 13:35

FLIP THE SWITCH

Determine today to look at everything through a lens of perfect love. And, list here First Corinthians chapter thirteen's 16 key points about what love is, employing and activating these points as your guide:

1. _____

2. _____

3. _____

4. _____

5. _____

6. _____

7. _____

8. _____

9. _____

10. _____

11. _____

12. _____

13. _____

14. _____

15. _____

16. _____

S-T-R-E-T-C-H

Who in your life has deeply hurt you? And how might you breach the wall of past sufferings and violations to love that person unconditionally? What can you do today to demonstrate/activate/manifest/*pour out your* unconditional love toward him or her?

REVIEW

1. Why is the "love chapter" (1 Cor. 13) so central to the operations of the gifts?

2. Which is most essential to the Christian life, faith or love?

3. Discerning of spirits is looking at anything in life through what?

4. Love has a unique quality in that it can cover what?

5. "Love literally gives us back the _____ to see each other without _____.

6. True or false? God forces us to love one another.

7. True or false? A mustard seed of faith is the best force to move mountains!

8. True or false? Love is something you have to ask God for.

JOURNAL

Increase your awareness of God's love for you in your everyday surroundings and functions. What reminders does He send you? Do you see Him in your difficult circumstance? In nature? In someone you meet? For the next week, record every concrete reminder of God's love. Determine to pursue Love.

PONDER/MEMORIZE

"And so we know and rely on the love God has for us." (1 John 4:16a). Personalize and declare it daily:

And so I KNOW and RELY on the LOVE God has for ME!

CHAPTER ELEVEN

Four Keys to Increasing Faith

TEACHING POINTS
FOUR KEYS:

1. Fasting & Prayer

2. Praying in the Spirit

3. Hearing the Prophetic Word of God

4. Fellowship

- Doors of Experience

- Entering in by faith

- Opening Doors

KEY CHAPTER SCRIPTURES

(in order of appearance in chapter)

Mark 11:24

Hebrews 11

2 Corinthians 5:7

Hebrews 4:2

Luke 17:5

Matthew 17:15-21

Jude 1:20

Romans 10:17

Ephesians 6:17

Romans 1:12b

James 2:14-18; 20-26

James 2:20-26

FLIP THE SWITCH

We walk by faith, not by sight! The key of faith is required to open the door to "see." It enables our spiritual eyes to see the unseen, that which is not in the natural. This type of faith requires an action on our part. It requires an entering into, by faith. A faith that puts the key into the lock, and turns the doorknob! Determine today not to be content only standing by the door listening in, enter in and see!

S-T-R-E-T-C-H

Initiate the building of your faith, so that He will increase your faith, and you will gain confidence! Determine and plan now when and how often you will fast, pray, listen, and fellowship, and stick to the plan!

REVIEW

1. True or false? Faith brings us into a biblical experience.

2. List ten examples of biblical truths that you can experience today, by faith!

    1. _____

    2. _____

    3. _____

    4. _____

    5. _____

    6. _____

    7. _____

    8. _____

9. _____

10. _____

3. We do not make spiritual decisions by what can be seen with _____ eyes.

4. Faith is only satisfied when one enters into the _____.

5. The sword of the spirit belongs to us, to wield as we please. True or false?

6. True or false? The Word alone will open doors for us.

JOURNAL

In what ways has your confidence/faith grown in your spiritual walk over the years? Can you identify the action/s you employed that were most effective? What worked for you? And, how else, in addition to the four keys, can you develop your faith?

PONDER/MEMORIZE

"Now faith is being sure of what we hope for and certain of what we do not see" (Hebrews 11:1).

I have an ENTIRE BOOK OF TRUTHS to enter INTO!

CHAPTER TWELVE

Biblical Meditation

TEACHING POINTS

- Biblical meditation and the imagination

KEY CHAPTER SCRIPTURES

(in order of appearance in chapter)

Proverbs 23:7

Philippians 4:8

Psalm 19:14; 104:34

2 Timothy 3:16-17; 4:14-15

Psalm 63:6

Revelation 19:10

Psalm 77:10-12; 143:5

Ephesians 1:18

Matthew 5:27-28

Job 33:14-16

Hebrews 4:12

John 6:63; 17:17

Colossians 3:3

Luke 11:11-13

Flip the Switch

Determine now to meditate on good things by choosing true, noble, just, pure, lovely, virtuous, praiseworthy, good report thoughts, because those thoughts will influence and transform you.

S-T-R-E-T-C-H

Read through your favorite Book of the Bible, or use the scripture references at the start of each chapter study as a starting point. As the Lord illuminates a verse to you, read it aloud, write it down, let it truly sink into your spirit. Carry it with you, repeat it as often as you can. Apply and incorporate that word into your day. Quote it to someone. Obey it. Ask God questions about it. Let it fuel your day! The key to memorizing a verse or passage is in its application, His word never falls void.

Review

1. Our thoughts manifest as the life that we live, true or false?

2. The testimony of Jesus is the spirit of _____.

3. What is the meditation organ of your spirit?

4. God can speak to us through our imagination. True or false?

5. The imagination realm releases actual realities in which realm?

6. How do we prevent the imagination from projecting things of the flesh?

7. Operating our imagination through biblical meditation can result in an interactive experience, true or false?

8. We can, by the spirit, enter into the reality of the Word.

9. When might it be dangerous to rely on our imagination?

10. True or False? Discernment by way of the imagination is invalid.

Journal

Can you recall good things you imagined as a child?

PONDER/MEMORIZE

I pray for the enlightening of the eyes of my heart in order that I can know the hope to which You have called Me Lord... (see Ephesians 1:18).

The WORD is alive and DWELLS in my SPIRIT!

CHAPTER THIRTEEN

Worship in Spirit and in Truth

TEACHING POINTS

- Tapping into the spiritual reality of worship

- Engaging

- Worshiping God as spirit beings

KEY CHAPTER SCRIPTURES

(in order of appearance in chapter)

John 4:19-20; 21-24

2 Corinthians 3:5-6

Revelation 1:10

2 Chronicles 5:13b-14

Amos 9:11

Acts 15:15-18

FLIP THE SWITCH

If you need a high level of breakthrough, strong worship is key, and you may see an incredible and sudden shift in your circumstances, as a result. Perhaps in the past, you have only experienced worship in the natural realm; determine now, to train yourself to worship in Spirit and in Truth.

S-T-R-E-T-C-H

The Lord said that when He, the Spirit of Reality, comes, He will guide you into all reality. Are you willing to be guided into all reality? God is restoring seers in the worship realm. Is your spirit willing? What steps can you personally take to make your spirit more willing?

Review

1. The word "truthfulness" can be translated as _____.

2. The Spirit of Truth is the Spirit of Reality, true or false? Why?

3. Everything has a spiritual reality, true or false?

4. What model of worship carries through from the Old Testament to the New? And what did God say He would do with it?

5. It doesn't matter how we worship God. True or False?

6. Only by _____ are we able to worship in spirit and truth.

7. Worship is primarily a:
   a) spiritual action
   b) physical action

8. We can worship God in any way we please. True or False?

Journal

Imagine yourself seated with Christ in the heavenly places described in Ephesians 2:6, and focus on that spiritual temple, worshiping God who is spirit, in the Throne Room, in Spirit and in Truth. Engage that part of you that is spirit by putting all of yourself into loving Him. Record your experience, in detail.

Ponder/Memorize

"Yet a time is coming and has now come when the true worshipers will worship the Father in spirit and truth, for they are the kind of worshipers the Father seeks. God is spirit, and His worshipers must worship in spirit and in truth" (John 4:23-24).

I CAN enter into an INTERACTIVE EXPERIENCE in WORSHIP anytime by FAITH!

CHAPTER · FOURTEEN

Entrusted with Secrets

TEACHING POINT

- The Lord shares/reveals His secrets to His people
- Becoming trustworthy as a prophet/seer
- Stewardship and accountability

KEY CHAPTER SCRIPTURES

(in order of appearance in chapter)

Amos 3:7

Genesis 18:17

John 10:27

1 Corinthians 4:1

Psalm 25:14

Isaiah 48:6

Matthew 11:25-26

Isaiah 42:9

1 Corinthians 2:9-10

Deuteronomy 29:29

Proverbs 25:2

Luke 16:10

Matthew 7:6

Genesis 37:8-11

Revelation 10:3-4

Judges 13:2-5; 16:17, 19

2 Kings 20:13-18

Hebrews 11:6

Flip the Switch

As you begin to move into seeing and the prophetic, the Lord will reveal more of His secrets to you. But it is not a one-way street, He values your, yes your input. In fact, He has given you incredible inner wisdom and knowledge. Are you leaning into God to hear His voice, sharpening your spiritual eyes to see what He is up to in the heavenly realms? Remember, Jesus could do nothing by Himself, only what He saw His Father doing, because "whatever the Father does the Son also does" (see John 5:19). *What can you do to lean in a little closer?*

S-T-R-E-T-C-H

The secret things belong to the Lord and He reveals them to whom He wills. He wants to share His secrets with you, but you have to have a faithful spirit able to conceal what you see, only sharing when He says it is okay. Some of what you see might not ever be shared, as a result. Not everyone can handle or understand what you might share in error, some might use the knowledge as ammo to destroy what God is trying to build in you or through you, and what you see, if the person is not able to handle it, could him or her. God needs to trust you, and people need to trust you too. Some things are just meant to be taken no further than God's throne in secret prayer and intercession. If you cannot understand what the Holy Spirit shows you, if you don't know whether you should keep it in your heart or share it, to be on the safe side, keep it in your heart and ponder it, as Mary pondered the messages given to her, and in time, you will have clarity. Also, do a heart self-check regarding pride, gossip, boastfulness, unforgiveness, ambition, a critical spirit, lust, hidden sin, and anything else that may endanger your ability to be faithful. It is also a good time to evaluate how obedient you've been, and resolve to improve in this area, if warranted. You will see much more than you ever dreamed possible, if you prove trustworthy.

REVIEW

1. What God shows you is always meant for everyone.

2. What happens if we share revelation we are not supposed to share?

3. What is a consequence of betraying God's trust?

4. King Hezekiah lacked discretion in revealing everything in his storehouses, even boasting that he didn't miss showing the Babylonian envoys even one thing. As a result of failing God's test of trust, what did the King lose?

5. True or false. Sharing with the wrong people may evoke unwelcome responses and reactions.

6. The true test of a prophet is not what he knows, but what he _____ knowing.

7. If you know God's secrets, you should also know how to _____ God's secrets

8. If I have the gift of prophecy and can fathom all mysteries and all knowledge, and if I have a faith that can move mountains, but have not_____, I am nothing" (1 Corinthians 13:2).

9. Love covers a multitude of _____.

JOURNAL

Has anyone ever betrayed your trust concerning a private matter? Have you been the target of gossip? Record how it made you feel. Did it change your direction for the worse? Did it destroy a plan? Did it negatively affect your heart? End a relationship? Cause confusion? Affect your resolve? Embitter you?

Ponder and write your thoughts about the following verse:

"Surely you desire truth in the inner parts; You teach me wisdom in the inmost place" (Psalm 51:6).

It is important not to share a secret about yourself with someone unless you have first shared it with God, to receive His take on the situation because sharing something with the world returns the world's take on the situation, its input, its opinion. The Truth comes from the hidden things the Holy Spirit has placed in your inward parts, where the Holy Spirit works those things into wisdom, and where it is protected from the enemy.

PONDER/MEMORIZE

"A gossip betrays a confidence, but a trustworthy man keeps a secret" (Proverbs 11:13).

I was created to know the DEEPER things of God!

CHAPTER FIFTEEN

Seers and the End of the World

TEACHING POINTS

- Testing the end-time prophecies according to the Word
- End-time theology
- Dangers

KEY CHAPTER SCRIPTURES

(in order of appearance in chapter)

1 Thessalonians 5:20-21

2 Peter 1:20-21

Galatians 1:8

1 John 4:1

Acts 17:11

2 Peter 1:20-21

FLIP THE SWITCH

What is your personal belief concerning the end times? Does your belief sway or slant your prophetic experiences? How does your theology measure up to the Word? Ask the Lord for discernment concerning this. What theologies concern you the most, and why?

S-T-R-E-T-C-H

Don't be swayed by false doctrines or teachings, and don't hold back in studying up on the subject of end times, because your understanding of the future will affect how you live day-to-day now.

Review

1. Prophetic experiences always confirm correct theology, true or false?

2. As credible as a leader might seem, he could still be way off on his theology, true or false?

3. A personal grid of theology might _____ a prophetic experience.

4. Prophecy never had its origin in human _____.

5. Jesus stripped satan of all his a._____ and b._____.

6. Which is not true? The Kingdom of God is like
   a. yeast
   b. a mustard seed,
   c. an oak tree

Journal

Think back upon a time, when you were misled. How did you discover the truth?

Ponder/Memorize

"Do not treat prophecies with contempt. Test everything. Hold on to the good" (1 Thessalonians 5:20-21).

I am CARRIED along by the Holy Spirit!

CHAPTER SIXTEEN

Seers and Spiritual Warfare

TEACHING POINTS

- Doctrines of demons
- Spiritual warfare: Identity, Authority, Triumph
- Maintaining our triumph over satan
- Enforcing and advancing
- Seer Orphans/Spiritual Maturity
- Core of Growth

KEY CHAPTER SCRIPTURES

(in order of appearance in chapter)

Acts 17:28

John 15:4

Ephesians 2:6

1 John 4:4

Matthew 16:19

1 John 5:11-12

Colossians 2:15

2 Corinthians 2:14; 5:20

Ephesians 6:19-20

Hebrews 2:14-15

Isaiah 14:16-17

John 8:43-44

2 Corinthians 10:3-6

1 Peter 5:8-9

John 8:32

Ephesians 6:11; 13-14

Philippians 3:16

Ephesians 1:17-18

Flip the Switch

Seek truth! Resist, and stand firm against the devil by standing firm in the faith. Determine to guard yourself against the devil's lies that seek to condemn you and prevent you from walking in the fullness of all that God has for you. Don't let the devil outwit you, be aware of his schemes that seek to cause you to abandon the faith and follow deceiving spirits.

S-T-R-E-T-C-H

Avoid becoming a seer orphan! How secure are you in your identity in Christ? The less you know about your position in Jesus Christ, the easier time of it for the devil to keep you spiritually and emotionally bound up, to make you spiritually blind. Don't become a seer orphan. Seeking God with everything in you to receive revelation and understanding of who God the Father says you are IN JESUS will greatly hinder satan's plans and cause you to walk in ever-increasing spiritual victory, because the authority you have as a believer in Christ is contained in your identity. He has given us His promises concerning our position in Jesus Christ to help wage more effective spiritual warfare against demonic powers, thereby actively applying the "shield of faith" (see Ephesians 6:16). Search out and study Bible promises concerning your identity to prevent satan from influencing your thought life, and as a hunger motivator to be more Christ like!

Review

1. Spiritual warfare revolves around

    1. _____

2. _____

3. _____

2. We are fighting for victory, or from victory?

3. Define the difference between victory and triumph

4. We are on earth as ambassadors doing what?

5. The God of peace will soon crush who under your feet?

6. Jesus stripped satan of all his a._____ and b_____ .

7. What does it mean to step out of Jesus' chariot?

8. Many seers struggle with identity issues, true or false?

9. We grow into what we have already _____ .

10. Understanding the glorious riches of our inheritance requires _____ .

11. a. Greater levels, greater devils?
    b. Or the more confidence in one's identity (thus authority) in Christ, the less spiritual warfare?

JOURNAL

Think back upon a time, where the Lord required you to press through a difficult circumstance, in which you celebrated the victory in triumph. How did it strengthen/motivate/encourage/ you for the next battle? Now think upon a current challenge, and imagine the triumph. How will you celebrate?

PONDER/MEMORIZE

"Be self-controlled and alert. Your enemy the devil prowls around like a roaring lion looking for someone to devour. Resist him, standing firm in the faith, because you know that your brothers throughout the world are undergoing the same kind of sufferings" (1 Peter 5:8-9).

I am fighting from Victory!

CHAPTER 1 7

Seer Orphans and Spiritual Maturity

NO STUDY NECESSARY

Conclusion:
From Glory to Glory

TEACHING POINTS

- Push forward for more
- Progression: a Kingdom Principle
- The nature of God's Relationship with us
- Restoring the gift of discerning of spirits

KEY CHAPTER SCRIPTURES

(in order of appearance in chapter)

Ezekiel 47:1-5

Isaiah 9:7

Matthew 13:31-33

Exodus 14:13-16

FLIP THE SWITCH

Move on! Raise your staff and stretch out your hand over the sea. Good counsel! Could God have opened the sea had Moses not raised his staff? For sure, God is sovereign, but usually, He requests our participation. What He asks of us is always something we can do, because He has given us the authority to do it. This is the case with the gift of discerning of spirits, it requires our participation, obedience, and willingness, our pressing in by faith. What can you do to press in for more!

S-T-R-E-T-C-H

Are your feet wet yet? By now, if you have gone through the lessons and activation sequences, you should be at least ankle-deep in exercising your spiritual eyes to see into the unseen realm, and in faithfully stewarding the secrets of the Lord entrusted to you. In no time at all, if you continue to press in, you will become increasingly established in your spiritual ability and gifting, and taking much ground in the process as a forerunner seer positioned to train the Body of Christ in the operation of the gift of discerning spirits, which is being restored to the Church.

REVIEW

1. For true unity to be restored to the Last Day's Church, what has to be restored?

2. What other gift, besides that of discernment has not yet been fully restored?

3. What are some of the signs of its restoration, things we are seeing now?

4. The nature of the Kingdom of God is to _____.

5. Which is not true? The Kingdom of God is like a. yeast, b. a mustard seed, c. an oak tree.

JOURNAL

How have you progressed? And what do you hope the Lord will show you in coming days?

PONDER / MEMORIZE

"And we, who with unveiled faces all reflect the Lord's glory, are being transformed into His likeness with ever-increasing glory, which comes from the Lord, who is the Spirit" (2 Corinthians 3:18).

I am RECEIVING the achievement that JESUS fulfilled!

—Answer Keys—

INTRODUCTION REVIEW ANSWER KEY

1. Temporary

2. All around us

3. A Christian who has begun to experience the supernatural realm but lacks solid biblical teaching, training, encouragement, and release

4. Counterfeiting

CHAPTER ONE
(THE MANTLE OF FIRE AND WATER)

Challenge Answer Key

1, Sovereign

2. Flipping the switch

3. Sovereign

4. Flipping the switch

5. Flipping the switch

6. Sovereign

Review Answer Key

1. Activate faith

2. Mantle: An anointing (see Luke 24:49)

3. True

4. True

5. True

Chapter Two
(Spiritual Senses)

Challenge Answer Key

1. The hope He has called us to

2. The riches of His glorious inheritance in the saints

3. The immeasurable greatness of His power toward us who believe

Review Answer Key

1. Seeing God

2. Focused on God

3. Distractions

4. Taste, touch, smell, sight, sound

5. Soul, physical

6. See the world; hear others, touch certain things, tasting certain things

7. Physical realm, interpersonal realm, spiritual realm

Chapter Three
(Impartation)

Review Answer Key

1. True

2. False

3. False

4. True

5. False (one should only impart what one possesses)

6. False (both Old and New Testaments)

7. True

8. False (it is symbolic of the Holy Spirit)

9. True, (you can only give what you have, but you can put it on God to give the double portion)

Chapter Four
(We Can All See)

Review Answer Key

1. False (because you can discern does not mean you have the "gift of" discerning of spirits or the appointment/office of seer. Review Ephesians 4:11.

2. True (see Ephesians 1:15-18).

3. False (We are commanded to heal the sick—Matthew 10:8).

4. True (see Hebrews 5:14).

Chapter Five
(Prophets and Seers)

Review Answer Key

1. True

2. True

3. False

4. True

Chapter Six
(The Unseen Realm)

Review Answer Key

1. True

2. Seen and unseen

3. Physical

4. Temporal

5. True

6. Unseen

7. True

8. False, it is neither good nor evil, it is merely a plane of existence where there can be good or evil.

Chapter Eight
(Discerning Spirits)

Review Answer Key

1. True

2. "The ability to distinguish," and "to test or prove."

3. Holy Spirit, heavenly spirits, the human spirit, and demonic spirits

4. Peter

5. Discern the spirits to accept new truth.

6. Angels and other heavenly creatures.

7. True

8. Eden

9. Carnal

10. False: Good or bad information

11. Love!

12. True

Chapter Nine
(Hindrances to Discernment)

Review Answer Key

1. Food, imagination.

2. Leaves our spirit open to the demonic, to defilement....

3. Guard your heart, understand your motive, prayerfully consider....

4. Extending forgiveness....

5. True

6. Hedge

CHAPTER TEN
(THE FORCE OF LOVE)

Review Answer Key

1. Because every spiritual gift has to be used in love

2. Through the eyes of Jesus

3. Sin

4. Eyes, sin

5. False. Love is a choice that we make.

6. Obedience to God's command to love one another is vital

7. False: Love is a greater force than hope or faith

8. False: A measure has been given to each one of us, we just have to stir it up!

CHAPTER ELEVEN
(FOUR KEYS TO INCREASING FAITH)

Review Answer Key

1. True

2. Salvation, healing, abiding, insight, power, joy, authority, hearing God, fruit of the Spirit, intimacy

3. Physical

4. Truth

5. False. It is the Holy Spirit's, and we must first submit to Him for maximum power and effectiveness.

6. False; without faith, doors will not open (unless God sovereignly opens them).

Chapter Twelve
(Biblical Meditation)

Review Answer Key

1. True

2. Prophecy

3. My imagination

4. True

5. The physical realm

6. Through biblical meditation, we can train our imagination to project/focus on the righteous things of the spirit.

7. True

8. True

9. When we are not close to Christ, if we are not pursuing Him, and spending time in His presence, in the Word, in prayer, and so on.

10. False

Chapter Thirteen
(Worship in Spirit and in Truth)

Review Answer Key

1. Reality

2. True

3. False, only that which is in the Holy Spirit is spiritual reality.

4. Worship in the Tabernacle of David. He would raise David's tent again.

5. False

6. Jesus, we engage the Father through the Son by the power of the Holy Spirit.

7. a. Spiritual

8. False, we must worship Him in Spirit and in Truth (John 4:23-24).

Chapter Fourteen
(Entrusted with Secrets)

Review Answer Key

1. False, sometimes God gives us revelation meant only for our ears

2. It can be turned and used against us

3. We become as weak as any other, giving the enemy an advantage

4. Just about all of his blessings

5. True

6. ....what he dies knowing.

7. Keep

8. Love

9. Sins

Chapter Fifteen
(Seers and the End of the World)

Review Answer Key

1. False, sometimes they do, but not always

2. True

3. Slant (influence)

4. Will (see 2 Peter 1:20-21)

CHAPTER SIXTEEN
(SEERS AND SPIRITUAL WARFARE)

Review Answer Key

1. Identity, authority, triumph

2. From

3. Victory is the win, triumph is the celebration

4. Enforcing and advancing the application of Jesus' victory

5. Satan

6. a. power; b; authority; c. is untrue

7. To step out of Jesus' chariot is to allow ourselves to listen to the voice of the devil and come into agreement with his lies. It is a position of defeat.

8. True

9. Received

10. Revelation

11. b.

CONCLUSION: GLORY TO GLORY

Review Answer Key

1. Restoration of the love of God

2. Gift of miracles

3. Healings, supernatural wonders, manifestations of God's glory

4. Progress

5. c.

Eyes of Honor

CHAPTER 1: MY STORY

Growing up, I spent my summers at an all-male Christian summer camp. Hiking, swimming, sports, archery, and horseback riding— this camp had it all. I have calculated that over the years I have spent close to a full year and a half at camp.

Even in this ideal environment, I constantly had young men come and ask for my input regarding how to handle their lustful thoughts. To think that we were completely removed from the presence of females for eight weeks, and yet these young Christian men—and I— still could not separate from the lustful thoughts that filled our minds.

One young man was even caught masturbating in the staff lounge and was sent home. Of course, it is easy to point the finger at how stupid that kid was. But, inside, many of us felt discouraged because the only difference between him and us was that we hid our sin better than he did.

Over the years, I have had hundreds of conversations in which other men have asked me how to deal with lustful thoughts. Even though I grew up with a solid Christian heritage in a homeschooling family, and despite the fact that I earned two masters degrees and the National Herald of Christ award, I lacked any real answers to offer my friends. I was caught in the same battle as the men who asked my input.

For years I have collected and read books on sexual purity, and yet I have not been satisfied by the answers offered to Christian men. I have heard better advice from my high school friend, Tom, who said, "When I feel tempted, I eat a raw potato. Nothing gets your mind off of naked ladies like eating a raw potato!"

I am not sure that Tom ever actually ate a raw potato, but his idea (though hilarious) is really not that different from the typical advice given to Christian men. Many Christian books try to help men through methods of *behavior modification*.

One of the most popular men's purity books of the last decade instructed men to "bounce" their eyes, meaning that one should look away from temptation before lustful thoughts take over.

While this advice might help a little bit, there must be a better answer. The men I have talked to about "bouncing" their eyes eventually found that they could hardly look an attractive woman in the face because of the fear of lusting. The bouncing-eyes approach sounds practical, but it does not reach the roots of lust.

This point was driven home for me while visiting a friend in southern California. We were at a burger joint when the inevitable conversation came up once again. He shared with me, "Jon, I have a beautiful wife, a couple of beautiful children, a wonderful job that provides well for us, a great home, and I couldn't be happier. Yet, I cannot get away from the lust in my eyes; I have talked to dozens of pastors and nobody seems to have answers. I appreciate that other men are honest enough to admit that they don't have answers, but when is someone going to get this figured out?"

At that point, a holy anger arose in my heart and I heard myself say out loud, "How is it that Jesus told us that we can raise the dead but Christian men can't even stop masturbating!" (See Matthew 10:8.)

Perhaps you have tried accountability, online filtering software, men's purity books, attending 12-step groups, or professional counseling, but to no avail. You may be holding this book in your hands wondering if this is going to be another waste of your time, or if, maybe, you have finally stumbled upon a book that has some real answers.

What Hasn't Worked

I am going to be real with you. This book contains what you need to be free of sexual temptation. I know that this is a big, almost surreal statement, yet I believe it to be true. Before I tell you what makes this book different, I will tell you what I have found in the books that are already on the market.

There are three main categories of books on the market regarding men's purity: 1) books that tell the reader how large the problem of lust is in our society, 2) books that tell a personal story of how the author ruined his whole life by following his lust, and 3) hard-to read books written by Christian psychologists which describe lust in clinical terms.

There is little variation regarding the approach to this topic. The majority of the books I have read essentially label lust as a disease and leave the Christian man with a weak, carnal answer regarding how to *manage* his disease. But this does not line up with the Word of God; when did Christ ever tell His followers to manage their sin?

May I be honest with you? Because I am writing to men who spend significant amounts of time each week battling lustful thoughts, this is going to be a raw book full of truth and brazenly honest feelings. I am not writing from an ivory tower of perfection. I have had my gutwrenching battles with temptation, and I have been cut and scarred in the warfare. But I have also come out as a victor. I have found through my personal experience and study of the Word that we can be free. Even though surveys have found that 82 percent of Christian men are privately struggling with lust,1 it doesn't have to be this way.

The aim of this book is not to put a Band-Aid on the problem; we must get to the roots of the infection. I want to give you hope: there is an antidote. Jesus did not save you from the bondage of 99 percent of your sins just to leave you struggling with lust for the rest of your life. This issue requires delving deeper into the hearts of men in order to finally bring health in this area.

The Accountability Myth

One of the first things I will tell you is that if you must have accountability, then you haven't really found the answer to your sin. Although accountability may help you manage your sin, it doesn't deal with the root. Jesus didn't provide us with complete freedom from the power of sin so that we could establish accountability groups to try not to sin. Jesus didn't have an accountability partner, and neither did the apostles.

I have a high regard for the interdependence of the Body of Christ; yet if we must lean on others *so as not to sin*, there is something fundamentally wrong with our theology. Clearly, the Bible teaches that we are the Body of Christ, and we are many interconnected members (see Rom. 12:5). This does not mean that we must create webs of accountability to keep each other from sinning. That is not taught in the Word.

This is where my approach comes in. I am not a pastor; I am not a counselor; I am not a psychologist. I am a student of the Word. I believe that the Bible has the answer. I also believe that the Bible is not complicated, and that when the Bible is complicated, it is probably being taught wrongly. The Bible is about relationship with God, and He would not want that to be complicated.

I carry a saying with me: *"Wrong teaching leads to wrong living; whereas right teaching leads to right living."* I believe that the struggle for sexual purity comes from wrong teaching. While most Christian men struggling with lust would be happy just to have victory over lust, I believe that the Lord has much more for us.

The Evidence Against Us

Right now the world is suffering from many evils regarding sexual sin. The sex industry worldwide is raking in over $57 billion a year. The sex slave trade is kidnapping, raping, and prostituting our sisters all around the world. Hollywood is ever increasing its degradation of women. Homosexual marriage, sex-change operations, and the abortion agenda are pushing forward in our society every day.

Although Christian leaders oppose these global sins, many continue in personal slavery to pornography, which has the same evil spirits behind it as the rest of these sins. They publically denounce the very spirits of lust and perversion to which they are privately enslaved. How will we ever take down the sex slave industry while we are in bondage to the same evil spirits that are behind it? The Bible's answer is simple:

> *...if My people, who are called by My name, will humble themselves and pray and seek My face and turn from their wicked ways, then will I hear from heaven, and I will forgive their sin and will heal their land* (2 Chronicles 7:14).

The world around us is sin-sick with a toxic poison of lust. The Church must first be healed of this toxicity before we can offer hope, healing, and restoration to a world trapped in sexual bondage. I interpret Second Chronicles 7:14 as saying, *when God's people stop focusing on those around them and deal with their own hearts, then God will bring healing to those around them as well.* God will heal the hearts of the homosexuals, abortionists, pornographers, and the like if, and when, we, as the Church, turn to Him, humble ourselves, and repent of our own sin.

Not only do 82 percent of Christian men regularly struggle with lust, but even those in the pulpit are suffering immensely. As a Church leader, I can say that it is very challenging to find someone safe to share your struggle with. Church leaders carry a heavy burden of expectation on their shoulders, and this makes it even harder to be open about failures and struggles. They fear losing their ministries and callings, so they keep their struggles secret, hoping to beat them on their own. Sadly, many of their stories end tragically. Considering this statistically, many in full-time ministry have been unfaithful to their spouses: "Forty percent of pastors have had extra marital affairs since entering the ministry."[3]

Those in the pulpit desperately need help too.

If we hope to fix the divorce rate inside the Church, we must find victory against lust. Lust isn't the only thing that causes marriages to fail, but it is almost always a factor. It is not just the sad, depressed, and angry people who are struggling with sexual temptation. "One study of 4,126 male business leaders, executives, and professionals reported that 88% of the men questioned had *at least* one affair."[4]

When we look at the numbers, the problem seems monumental. Yet I believe Jesus has given us a genuine solution that will bring actual freedom to the Church. If we can get freedom from sexual sin inside the Church, then we will begin to have a healing impact on the sin-sick world around us.

The Methods I Tried

On my journey to freedom from sexual bondage, I found that the Church offered many methods for finding freedom. I spent time vigorously trying each of the methods and found limited or temporary freedom. Having exhausted every avenue that I could, I turned to the Lord in my frustration and cried out for true, full, and lasting freedom. I knew that I needed freedom not only for myself, but also for the host of other men struggling in the Body of Christ.

The following are a few of the methods promising freedom that I tried. Perhaps you haven't tried these, and I can forewarn you of certain weaknesses; maybe you are trying these paths and feel like there is more freedom available; or perhaps you have tried them and are discouraged. If you are a part of the third group, be encouraged, because Jesus—the Author and Perfecter of your faith (see Heb. 12:2 NASB)—is going to continue working in your life to bring you to fullness of freedom.

Deliverance From Demonic Oppression

When I first began to feel trapped by pornography, my first thought was that I must be in bondage to a demon of lust. As a Christian, I had heard about demons for many years and thought that I must need deliverance.

I read every book on deliverance that I could find. Here is what I found to be true. The devil is a totally defeated foe and a tremendous liar. After the cross of Christ, the only way the devil can gain power is by getting individuals to agree with his lies. As I began to understand that I had come into agreement with his lies, I worked through deliverance and found a measure of freedom, but I knew there was a greater freedom than what I was experiencing.5

Dealing with the Soul

After I realized that I didn't just need a demon cast out of me, I began to look at my emotional life. I was looking for how my life could have become so out of control. I came across the book *The Spiritual Man* by Watchman Nee. Because I had heard so many good things about this book, I hungrily read it, twice in fact!

I began to believe that my lust was a product of my soul not being submitted to my spirit. So I worked as hard as possible to bring my soul into subjection to my spirit. It was many wasted years later that a dear brother showed me the error of this concept. I have devoted a whole chapter to taking apart this myth, but suffice it to say here that *the soul is a good thing that should not be suppressed.* If you have been caught in the "submit your soul to your spirit" teaching, consider reading *Escaping Dualism* by Harold Eberle.

Dualism: The Human Condition

I moved from trying to suppress my soul to instead trying to crucify my fleshly, carnal nature. I began to think that I must "die daily" like the apostle Paul said in his letter to the Corinthians (see 1 Cor. 15:31). Perhaps my problem was my sin nature. I just needed to deny self and pick up my cross. I became focused on my cross and tried to be my own executioner.

After many years of frustration, discouragement, and extensive biblical study, my eyes were opened to this truth: *My crucifixion with Christ is a past-tense, accomplished fact that I can add nothing to.* I cover this in much more detail in a later chapter.

Internet Filters

While a filter may be a helpful preventive tool, it is not a solution. Placing a filter on your mobile phone or computer may help block Internet pornography, but if you must have this, then you have not actually removed the lust from your heart.

Internet filters are like childproofing a home; once the child is grown, you do not need to have a childproof home. In the same way, once you have dealt with removing lust from your heart, Internet filters become unnecessary.

Introspection

At this point in my journey, I was not looking for demons, I was not trying to suppress my soul, and I was not trying to crucify myself, so I dug deeper into introspection. I figured that I must begin to "take every thought captive" (see 2 Cor. 10:5). I set a mental guard and filtered my thoughts on a constant basis. It did not take long in this stage for me to begin to feel tired and burnt out. I was working and struggling as hard as I could, but I ended up crying out in my heart like Paul did in Romans 7:24: *"O wretched man that I am! Who will deliver me from this body of death?"* (NKJV).

The Lord began to show me that the focus of introspection was *self*. Knowing that *"the heart is deceitful above all things, and it is exceedingly corrupt..."* (Jer. 17:9 WEB), how could I trust the assessment I gained from my own heart about my own heart! Introspection was draining my life and getting me nowhere. *I realized that I had placed my focus on myself, rather than turning my focus toward Jesus and His grace.*

Inner Healing

I knew that the Lord was saying that I needed to focus on Him and not myself, but I didn't really know how to do that. And because I was incapable of taking all my thoughts captive, I began to wonder where these thoughts were coming from. I began to look for the roots of my thought life in the experiences and memories that I had accumulated over the years. I did find a new measure of success against lust by working through my memories with repentance and forgiveness.

Unfortunately, I began to feel like I would never reach the bottom of my bucket. I realized that forgiveness and repentance took me from negative 100 back to ground zero; but the Word of God describes a life that is lived at positive 100. Inner healing was very helpful, it helped me deal with the past, but I still didn't have my identity straightened out for walking forward.6

The Clinical Approach

Eventually, I sought out Christian counseling with a focus on those caught in sexual bondage. I reasoned that because they work with people with similar issues all the time, then they must have found a way to help people. I submitted to analysis and spent some time in the office of a world-class expert in this arena. I was very excited when I first sat down with him. I thought, "I am in the one place that probably has the answers I have been searching for. I am finally going to find answers!"

Unfortunately, this was the most disappointing point in my journey. Much of modern Christian counseling has been putting Band-Aids on major infections. Having searched and even gone to the top of the sexual purity mountain in search of answers, I was shocked and disappointed to find nothing of the true freedom I sought.

The main three tools incorporated by the clinical approach were completely secular in approach. They are as follows:

Tool 1: Labeling

As I submitted to the professional counselor, I was given a host of labels regarding my bondage to sexual sin. Rather than reinforcing the labels that God has given me—son, beloved, righteous, light of the world, salt of the Earth, royalty, and so forth—the clinical approach placed psychological labels over my sin. Rather than the biblical fact that I was in bondage to the sin of lust, I was labeled with a "disease" called "sexual addiction." I have a problem with this because I can repent of a sin, but I can't repent of a disease.

Also the counselor went on to claim that once a person is an addict, that person is always an addict. I have a problem with this also because he whom the Son sets free is free indeed (see John 8:36). Yet according to this counseling model, even if people do find a measure of freedom, they are considered to be in recovery for the rest of their lives.

I cannot imagine the apostle Paul sitting in a dank church basement talking about how he has been a recovering murderer for 20 years. Men, is this the level of freedom we are willing to accept simply because nobody has anything better to offer?

Tool 2: Motivating Factors

The tool that was used for motivation in the hands of the clinical approach was mainly fear: to be more specific, the fear of punishment. The counselor had each individual write up punishments that he would use on himself if he operated in lust. For example, "If I view pornography, I will give $100 to a political cause I don't believe in."

Over my years of study in the Word, I have found that there are only two ways to live—in love or in fear. *"There is no fear in love. But perfect love drives out fear, because fear has to do with punishment. The one who fears is not made perfect in love"* (1 John 4:18). Because we Christians know that we are called to walk in love, we cannot allow fear to be a part of our lives.

Punishment and fear are never healthy ways to motivate walking in true love; this would be like threatening children by saying that they must love you or else you will mercilessly beat them. The only way that children can learn to walk in love is through our displaying love to them as an example to follow. That is what God has done for us. *"We love Him because He first loved us"* (1 John 4:19 NKJV). And Romans 2:4 says that it is His kindness that brings us to repentance, not fear of punishment, guilt, or condemnation.

The idea that counselors could hang the fear of punishment over people's heads in the hopes of motivating them to walk in love was especially surprising and absurd. Jesus was the one who said, "If you love Me, you will obey Me" (see John 14:15). Therefore, love is the motivator for godly obedience, not fear.

Tool 3: Behavior Modification

The ability to force internal change through external pressure is a total myth. Imagine pushing a basketball underwater inside a swimming pool; the harder you push down, the more force the ball has in trying to surface. This is just as futile as the cycles of punishment that the clinical approach has adopted.

I was given a rubber band to put on my wrist and told to snap myself every time I had a lustful thought. I was told that I was totally powerless against my addiction/disease and that I would have to physically retrain my body and mind to walk in freedom. Christian counseling promised me that external regulations and behavioral modifications would be able to keep my sin nature in check. But this is not the *"free indeed"* (John 8:36) that Jesus promised. And I was not willing to settle for this nonsense.

I remember sitting next to "John" in a Sex Addicts Anonymous group when he shared that he had been in recovery for 14 years and that he had been sober (had not masturbated) for two years. The man on the other side of John congratulated him and asked him why he didn't seem happy about such an accomplishment.

Then John broke down in tears and exclaimed, "I have been at these meetings multiple times a week for 14 years. I have been sober for two years, but I do not feel any freer! I still constantly have lustful thoughts and view women in evil ways. I want to be changed inside, but the behavioral modifications have only changed my outside reality, not my inside struggle. I don't want to go on like this."

"John" is like many Christian men. He has tried everything the Church has had to offer, but is in a state of despair that the methods and the freedom that have been offered him are far below the freedom that the Bible promises. Personally, I believe the Bible has the answers that men have been longing for in this area for many years. It is time to dig deep and lay the axe to the root of this bondage once and for all!

Identity Shift

My approach to lasting freedom is based on changing the identity of the one in bondage to lust. As you read this book, you will find that your understanding of identity will be challenged. You will be stretched doctrinally and experientially. You will need to make major shifts in heart and mind.

Most people have formed their identity around their actions: "I do plumbing; therefore, I am a plumber." "I sin; therefore, I am a sinner." "I can't stop thinking lustful thoughts; therefore, I am a sex addict."

The truth is that your identity is not the sum total of your actions; identity is the foundation of your life from which your actions flow. For example, if you were born and raised in Spain, then your identity is that of a Spanish citizen who most likely speaks Spanish. Identity comes before actions, and actions flow forth from identity. Rightly stated: "I am righteous in Christ; therefore, I live righteously." *Identity always precedes actions.*

Identity is made of three components: the mind, the heart, and revelation. The mind represents all of the thinking that a person has processed. The heart contains all of the experiences that a person has had. Revelation is the place where the heart and mind have come into agreement to form a foundational belief system. *Identity flows out of a person's revelation.*

Imagine, for example, a young boy who is told every day that he is worthless. Certain thoughts form in the boy's mind. Also, if the boy is slapped and abused regularly, the experiences are stored within his heart. The combination of his heart and mind leads to a revelation that says, "You are worthless. You are trash. You don't matter. Your actions don't matter. There is no God. You should just do whatever you want because nobody will hold you accountable." And on the basis of this revelation, the identity of a criminal flows forth!

Biblically, we can observe how this identity transition took place in the life of Saul of Tarsus. On the road to Damascus, Saul had a revelation of Jesus that challenged his heart and mind—he had a tremendous experience that left him blind for three days (see Acts 9:1-30). I would imagine that in those three days he had his heart and mind come into agreement to form a new foundational belief system—one founded on the truth that Jesus is the Christ.

His new revelation caused him to have a new identity so that, after this shift, he was willing to die for Christ, whereas four days earlier he had been willing to kill those who believed in the Christ. It is amazing how quickly people's identities can change when their hearts and minds align and form a new revelation.

If identity flows out of revelation, then to change your identity, you must get a new revelation! To get a new revelation, you first have to renew your mind with truth and allow new experiences into your heart. This book and the tools within are designed to give you the truths and experiences you need to receive a new revelation and identity.

Tool

Which of the following paths have you tried? Based on a scale of effectiveness from one to ten (one indicating extreme ineffectiveness and ten signifying extreme effectiveness), how would you rate your experience?

Deliverance

Suppressing the soul

Battling the flesh nature

Internet filtering

Introspection

Inner healing

Managing your sexual appetite

12-step approach

Professional counseling

Ready for something better?

ENDNOTES

1. "In his book, *The Sexual Man*, Dr. Archibald Hart revealed the results of a survey of some 600 Christian men on the topic of masturbation: 61% of married Christian men masturbate; 82% of these have self sex on an average of once a week; 10% have sex with self 5-10 times per month, 6% more than 15 times per month, and 1% more than 20 times a month. [Thirteen percent] of Christian married men said they felt it was normal." Passage quoted from: Mike Genung, "Statistics and information on pornography in the USA," *Blazing Grace*, 2005, http://www.blazinggrace.org/cms/bg/pornstats (accessed March 14, 2011).

2. "SeXXX Business Statistics," *Cross Cultural Connections*, http:// crosscultural-connections.org/documents/sex_stats.pdf (accessed March 14, 2011).

3. "Pastors and Adultery," *Gay Christian Movement Watch*, http://www.gcmwatch .com/4752/pastors-and-adultery (accessed March 14, 2011).

4. Thomas F. Fischer, "The Affair-Proof Pastorate," http://www.ministryhealth .net/mh_articles/294_affair_proof_pastorate.html (accessed March 14, 2011).

5. For more on deliverance, I highly recommend reading *Victory Over the Darkness* by Neil T. Anderson.

6. I have found Wellspring Ministries in Anchorage, Alaska to be a tremendous ministry for inner healing.

Normal Christianity

CHAPTER ONE: WHAT IS NORMAL?

What is the normal Christian life? We do well at the outset to ponder this question. The object of these studies is to show that it is something very different from the life of the average Christian. —Watchman Nee[1]

In 1886, Doctor John Pemberton, a pharmacist from Atlanta, Georgia, created the first batch of Coca-Cola. Dr. Pemberton concocted the formula in a three-legged brass kettle in his backyard. The name was a suggestion given by John Pemberton's bookkeeper, Frank Robinson. Being a bookkeeper, Frank Robinson also had excellent penmanship, and it was he who scripted "Coca-Cola" into the flowing letters of the famous company logo. The soft drink was first sold to the public at the soda fountain in Jacob's Pharmacy in Atlanta. Since its humble beginnings, Coca Cola has become world famous. Currently, more than 1.6 billion servings of Coca-Cola are consumed every day in more than 200 countries. The company has been in business for well over 100 years, employing nearly 100,000 people around the world.[2]

This amazing rags-to-riches story begs the question, how does a product become such a market force that almost anywhere in the world you can find its influence? The short answer, *it tastes good.*

This is not a book about soda and its influence in the world. Having traveled extensively, I am conscious of the sad fact that there are many people familiar with Coca-Cola, even in deeply remote areas, who have never heard the name of Jesus.

How is it that the name of Jesus, which has had 2,000 years to spread, has not yet reached the whole world, whereas a soft drink can reach the world in 100 years? Even with approximately 500,000 churches in the United States of America, the Great Commission (see Matt. 28:19-20) has not yet been fulfilled. Why is this so? The short answer, *our Christianity doesn't taste good.*

In 1985, Coke decided to alter its secret formula. Coke had been slipping behind their competitor, Pepsi, and thought the answer would be found in a new blend. Coke's chief executive officer announced, "The best has been made even better!" But the announcement triggered a furor. Within days they were re-thinking their re-think. Coca-Cola reintroduced the old formula, calling it "Classic Coke." Within months, Classic Coke had overtaken Pepsi.3

When the original recipe, given by Jesus Himself, is altered, Christianity becomes undesirable. Fortunately, the Church is coming into a significant shift in the years ahead, restoring her to what I have termed "Normal Christianity." In this book, you will be re-presented with the original recipe that Jesus gave His Church. As a wise company once said, "You can't beat the real thing!"

Revival

Christians from all walks of life often declare that what the Church really needs is a "revival." This is a statement that always brings a sly smile to my face. Please understand that there is no disdain in this look, merely the inquisitive entertainment that I enjoy from having heard hundreds of varied explanations of what the word *revival* means.

As I have traveled and ministered in many different denominations, I have heard countless definitions of *revival*. Gathering the many answers to "what is revival" has in some ways become a hobby of sorts. Over time, I have devised a way of understanding the opinions I have heard, placing them on a sliding scale.

My scale runs from 1-10, 1 being denominations considered conservative in doctrine and practice, typically the historic denominations (about 1.3 billion individuals worldwide).4 When asked to define revival, an individual from this background will typically give a concise definition similar to this: *Revival is when God comes close to the Church and Christians repent of their hidden sins and non-Christians are convicted of their sins in the streets and cry out to God for salvation.* As one individual from this end of the scale stated to me, *"Revival is community awareness of God."* I summarize this viewpoint as God spontaneously coming close to the Church and people getting saved at an unusual rate. This is usually attributed to repentance of sin, which is somewhat confusing because then it is both the cause and effect of revival.

Now consider the perspective of the 10 on my scale. Here the denominations are of the Pentecostal or Charismatic type (about 707 million individuals worldwide).5 When an individual from this end of the scale is asked to define *revival,* it is a much more complex phenomenon. First of all, the definition would be inclusive of everything on the scale from 1-9 and much more. This definition of *revival* includes the following: raising the dead, casting out demons, healing the sick, walking on water, multiplying food, power evangelism, angelic visitations, transport in the spirit between locations, as well as all nine of the Holy Spirit's gifts in operation. These experiences are major marks of what those on this scale of 10 define as *revival.*

In the past few years, I have noticed that Christians in this group have become so burned out on using the word *revival* that many of the leaders have started using new terms to communicate more specifically. Words such as: *cultural transformation, renewal, outpouring, reformation, restructuring, new wineskin,* and so on. Rather than throwing my personal definition on the pile, I have arrived at a conclusion. *I do not believe in revival!*

No matter where you are on the scale, most likely you are stunned by that statement, because every denomination believes in revival by some definition. I propose a totally different approach. Having looked at the Gospels and the Book of Acts, I would say that everything on the scale is expected of every Christian. It does not matter where you fit on the scale, God expects the Normal Christian to live as a 10 and more. In short, the New Testament does not present the idea of revival; it shows what a *Normal Christian* life looks like.

I know that this concept runs against the grain of many years of Protestant teaching. But as the late Walter Martin said, "Controversy for the sake of truth is a divine command."6 We must break free from the wrong concepts that are holding us back.

Jesus and the Book of Acts are the standard of Normal Christianity. Remember the fad a few years ago when people wore bracelets reminding them, *"What Would Jesus Do?"* Christians state that Jesus is the example of how to live, yet this has been limited in many cases to how we view our moral character. When Christians tell me that they want to live like Jesus, I like to ask if they have multiplied food, healed the sick, walked on water, raised the dead, paid their taxes with fish money, or calmed storms. I typically receive bewildered looks, but that's what it is like to live like Jesus!

Perhaps we are ignoring a large portion of what living like Jesus really includes. While I agree that we are to live like Jesus, *"Those who say they live in God should live their lives as Jesus did"* (1 John 2:6 NLT). I am also aware that the application of Jesus' model has been minimized to something that can be accomplished by living a moral life. Many Christians believe that they can live like Jesus without ever operating in the supernatural. *Does that sound right to you after reading in the Bible about all of the miracles He performed?*

No Such Thing

If a group of Christians in a region began to seriously live like Jesus, in the full meaning of that reality, the rest of the Church would elevate them and claim that a sovereign move of God is taking place. When this happens, it creates an unfortunate separation that lessens the responsibility of the rest of the Church to also live like Jesus in fullness. When we see revival as a spontaneous phenomenon that happens randomly, we show our lack of understanding of the true nature of Christianity. We must begin to see that everything that has been defined as revival is considered normal by the Bible. As author Graham Cooke has said so well:

> Unlike inhabitation, there is no call for revival found anywhere in Scripture. The Church, quite simply, should never need reviving. Revival is not about getting people saved; revival is about the Church coming back to her original purpose before God. I think it's very sad that so many of us have prayed and longed for revival—it means the Church is a long way from what God wants us to be. Maybe, just maybe, a little touch from God could bring us immediately into line. That's the mystery of life with the Godhead—you just never know what could turn the tide of history.7

Consider the question, "How many revivals are in the Book of Acts?" This question is fundamentally flawed. My contention is that there is no such thing as revival in the New Testament; therefore, the answer is none. *Revival* is merely a word that has developed into many complicated interpretations. Yet the result has actually distanced the Church from what she is called to be. There are many interpretations that state, "The Church will be like Jesus when revival comes," which actually removes from our shoulders the burden of living like Jesus in the present.

Once more, everything that we have called revival, the New Testament teaches as Normal Christianity. I believe in Normal Christianity. Next I will explain the definition of two terms that will be used throughout this book: *Normal Christianity* and *Average Christianity*.

Normal and Average

Average is a mathematical form of estimating. Let's say that Farmer John sells bushels of apples, and last week he sold 10 bushels. To find the average number of apples per bushel, you must add up the total number of apples, and then divide by the number of bushels, in this case, 10. This is how you arrive at an average of let's say 40 apples per bushel. Now if we were to take this a step further and say that Farmer Steve sold 15 bushels containing 50 apples each, this would mean that Farmer John is selling fewer apples on average than Farmer Steve.

Normal is a completely different system of measurement. Normal is based on comparing with an ideal. For example, a normal human being has 10 fingers and 10 toes. Notice that I am not saying that the *average* human being has 10 fingers and 10 toes, but a *normal* human being has these. That is because we are comparing all human beings against the concept of an ideal human being. The normal human being has two eyes, a nose, a mouth, and so forth. If a person were to be lacking in any of these areas, that person would not be considered below average, rather, that person would be abnormal. Abnormal means that there is an aberration from the standard of what is considered normal. Jesus Christ is the example of Normal for the Christian. To be different from Jesus in any way is to be an aberration from the standard set by His life.

Most Christians process their lives through averages, comparing their spirituality against the backdrop of neighbors, friends, their church family members, and relatives. When describing the type of church that they attend, typically comparisons are used for description. *"My church has great worship compared to the church I used to attend. My pastor gives boring sermons, not good ones like our youth pastor. We have a huge church, compared to the other ones in town."* The comparisons are endless. When describing revival, current spirituality (below average) is compared with what is described as revival (above average spirituality).

Consider how your mind automatically answers the following questions:

- Are you frequently angry?

- Do you have a lot of lustful thoughts each day?

- Do you swear often?

- Do you read your Bible enough?

- How strong is your prayer life?

The answers to these questions do not matter for my point to be made, but consider *how* you arrived at your answers. Most likely you arrived at your answers by comparison. Perhaps you compared with what you know of the people around you or the people who you look up to (or look down on). Maybe you even compared your current state to that of yourself in the past. Each of these ways of arriving at your answer reveals that you are thinking in the system of averages.

If you arrived at your answers by looking at Jesus as the example—He is the only measuring rod for your life—then you are one of very few people who think this way. This is the shift in thinking that we all must make: Jesus is the only measuring rod for what is considered Normal Christianity. If our lives do not resemble the life of Jesus, then the only definition for us is abnormal.

As long as we allow the wrong system of measurement, we will forever make the same error as the homeowner in the following Chinese proverb.

One day a man wanted to install a pipe on his oven. He measured the length with his ruler and asked the coppersmith to make a ten-foot long pipe. When the pipe was delivered, it seemed to be a foot too long. It would not fit. He reprimanded the coppersmith for the mistake. The coppersmith measured it again with his own ruler and found it was exactly ten feet. But the customer insisted that it was a foot too long.

Finally, the coppersmith examined the customer's own ruler and discovered that it was sawed off a foot. The customer's child had done this as he was playing with this ruler. No wonder, then, that the measurement always ended up a foot longer.

Our systems of spiritual measurement are like this ruler, an untrustworthy standard. We must reorient all standards of measurement and look only at Jesus as the ideal. He is the only One against whom we should compare ourselves. He is Normal, and either we are Christlike, or we are abnormal. These are our only options. We must no longer get a false sense of comfort by comparing averages and perhaps finding that we are above average in our spirituality. Many above-average Christians are still abnormal. When we mistake average for normal, we end up far below what God established through Jesus as Normal.

Normal Is a Personal Responsibility

All revivalists, both past and present, have carried a high level of personal responsibility to live as Normal Christians, with Jesus as their role model. Revival is not something in outer space that must be drawn to earth through the right formula of actions. Revival does not even exist; it is merely a term for describing Christians actually living like Jesus. If we are going to shift out of the mindset of occasionally living like Jesus and call it revival, we must be willing to accept the fact that we are required to live as Normal Christians every day. This is our responsibility and is not contingent upon something sovereign that takes place outside of us. The question has never been, "Where is revival?" but the question should have always been, "Who is revival?" You and I are the answer to that question.

As a Normal Christian, I am revival (if we must use this term); revival is not something that occurs outside of me. Proverbs 26:20 says, *"Without wood, a fire goes out...."* Normal Christians pay close attention to the fire of their own spirits and are constantly gathering wood and feeding the flame of the Holy Spirit. Maintaining your own spirit and the fire of the Holy Spirit within you is how you sustain revival.

It is a major shift to understand that revival is a personal responsibility to live like Jesus. But it is the renewing of the mind that will lead to permanently sustained revival. Revival is not a matter of finding and implementing the correct formula. It is a matter of right perspective and lifestyle.

An Average Christian is like a *thermometer,* in that he or she can describe the spiritual climate to you. Normal Christians, however, are like *thermostats* because everywhere they go, they shift the atmosphere. Consider Jesus, the first Normal Christian, after the wedding at Cana (the beginning of His ministry). He was never again able to walk into any atmosphere and be a wallflower. Normal Christians affect change in every environment. This type of lifestyle is not accidental; it requires constant, personal responsibility.

I have found that one of the heaviest challenges to being normal is living in the present. Typically we want to worship at the altar of our past experiences, revivals, and the good ol' days, or we want to prophesy and declare about the future move of God. But the responsibility of living normal in the present is extremely unpopular. It is vital that we take up our personal responsibility every day, no matter the circumstances that surround us. The famous Normal Christian, Charles Finney, was once asked to define *revival*. He stated that revival is as simple as drawing a circle on the ground around yourself; within that circle, you have a revival.

Normal Is Appealing

Many strategies have been implemented to make Christianity more appealing to the secular realm. Perhaps a funnier sermon, a new coat of paint, better music, a casually dressed pastor, and the list goes on—all in an attempt to re-present the Gospel in Above-Average packaging. What would happen if we were to throw out the standard ideas of Average thinking and try Normal thinking?

Think for a minute about the ministry of Jesus. He didn't have a building; He didn't have funny sermons, PowerPoint, music, and the like. Yet, Jesus had massive crowds. He was beloved of sinners, the government did not want to bother Him, and the only people who wanted to kill Him were the religious folks. The religious live comparing themselves with each other, and Jesus totally devastated their personal assessments because no Pharisee could ever measure up to Him. Jesus' life impossibly raised the average, and it made them all look bad. Shockingly, Jesus claimed to have set the *low bar* of what a Normal Christian is to be, *"I tell you the truth, anyone who has faith in Me will do what I have been doing. He will do even greater things than these, because I am going to the Father"* (John 14:12).

Average Christianity is rampant in the European and North American churches. Statistically, this is the most unattractive form of Christianity in the entire world. But back when Christians were normal, Simon the Sorcerer would have paid money to have what Peter had (see Acts 8). Sinners wanted to be with Jesus, but nowadays the world does not want to be with His followers. As Mahatma Ghandi put it so frankly, "I like your Christ. I do not like your Christians. Your Christians are so unlike your Christ."8 We are called to be little-Christs, which is what the name Christian means. Normal Christianity is the most attractive thing in the entire universe. In the following quote, Watchman Nee describes the beauty of Normal Christianity.

From the Holy Scriptures we may see that the life as ordained by God for Christians is one full of joy and rest, one that is uninterrupted communion with God, and is in perfect harmony with His will. It is a life that does not thirst and hunger after the world, that walks outside of sins, and that transcends all things. Indeed, it is a holy, powerful and victorious life, and one that constitutes knowing God's will and having continuous fellowship with Him.

The life which God has ordained for Christians is a life that is hid with Christ in God. Nothing can touch, affect or shake this life. As Christ is unshakable, so we are unshakable. As Christ transcends all things, we also transcend all things. As Christ is before God, so we are before Him. Let us never entertain the thought that we should be weak and defeated. There is no such thing as weakness and defeat; for "Christ is our life" as declared in Colossians 3:4. He transcends all; He cannot be touched by anything. Hallelujah! This is the life of Christ!

The life ordained for Christians is full of rest, full of joy, full of power, and full of the will of God. But let us inquire of ourselves as to what sort of life we are living today. If our life is not what God has ordained it to be, then we need to know victory. Hence, we shall look into this matter of our experience. And what we shall relate here may not be pleasing to our ears, because some of us are rather pathetic; yet we need to humble ourselves in order that we may see our lack and receive grace from God.9

What a beautiful description of Normal Christianity! I would like to build on Nee's thought by adding the supernatural element of the Normal Christian life as found in the New Testament. Every sentence in the next three paragraphs is paraphrased from Scripture. This is how the Bible describes Normal Christians:

Every normal Christian has a spiritual river of water flowing from their innermost being. This is the same river that flows from the throne of God and brings life and healing to the nations. This water quenched all their spiritual hunger. They now carry a fountain of water that releases eternal life everywhere that they go. They had each had an encounter and experience with the almighty God where they went through a mystical transformation of being born again. They were given the very mind of Christ. They walked as new creatures on this earth, as partakers of the divine nature. When they spoke, they considered their words to be the very oracles of God. They had prayer meetings where the whole building was shaken by the power of God. Their shadows falling on people caused healing to happen. Articles of their clothing were healing diseases, and they had so many ordinary miracles that they had to come up with a category of miracles called *extra ordinary*. One of the Church leaders even rebuked them for acting like mere humans.

Their perspective was that they were seated in heavenly places, ambassadors sent from Heaven as representatives of God to bring reconciliation to all humankind. Everybody in the Church was considered a king and a priest, as well as a citizen of Heaven. The almighty Creator of the universe was known to them by other names, such as Friend, Beloved, and Daddy. When they performed miracles, sorcerers wanted that level of power so badly that they offered money for it. When they were persecuted and jailed, angels freed them from prison.

They had gatherings of people who were so hungry for God that they would meet all night—someone even died by falling out a window, and then they raised him from the dead. Then there was the time when a viper bit one of them on the hand and the poison didn't harm him at all; in fact, he held it over a fire until the snake fell off. They walked in so much spiritual power and authority that the Holy Spirit had to block them from going on one of their mission trips. This is what many of us would consider a revival of astronomical proportions, but I am convinced that according to the Bible, this is Normal Christianity.

Activation

At the end of each of the following chapters, there is an Activation section. The activation suggests an exercise that will help you put the truth of the chapter into practice. These are basic exercises intended to stretch your spiritual muscles and prepare you to walk as a Normal Christian. The truths in this book are deep and stretching. In order to get the most out of it, I strongly recommend that at the end of each chapter you stop, put in your bookmark, and complete the activation exercise. You will receive the best absorption of this material if you do. Most of all, enjoy and have fun growing!

Acknowledgment

Also at the end of the following chapters, I acknowledge people who have helped shape my spiritual life. I know it's not "normal" to intersperse these thank-yous throughout the book, but considering the focus of each chapter, it just seems right to do so.

I would like to personally thank Pastor Bill Johnson of Bethel Church in Redding, California. Your tireless work has taught a generation how to be truly Normal Christians. Your teaching has fed my spirit like none other, and I thank the Lord for you.

ENDNOTES

1. Watchman Nee, *The Normal Christian Life* (Fort Washington, PA: Christian Literature Crusade, 1975), 9.

2. http://www.thecoca colacompany.com/ourcompany/index.html; accessed February 8, 2011.

3. "Coke dropping 'Classic' tagline from logo" *MSNBC*; http:// www.msnbc.msn.com/id/28932986/ns/business consumer_news; accessed March 23, 2011.

4. "Religions of the World"; http://www.religioustolerance.org/ worldrel.htm; accessed March 10, 2011.

5. James Rutz, *Mega Shift, Igniting Spiritual Power* (Colorado Springs, CO: Empowerment Press, 2005), 25-27.

6. Walter R. Martin, quoted on *The Quotable Christian;*http://www. pietyhilldesign.com/gcq/quotepages/truth.html; accessed February 28, 2011.

7. Graham Cooke, *Drawing Close* (Grand Rapids, MI: Chosen Books, 2003),16.

8. Mohandas Gandhi, quoted on *Brainy Quote;* http://www. brainyquote.com/quotes/quotes/m/mohandasga107529.html; accessed February 9, 2011.

9. Watchman Nee, *The Life That Wins* (New York: Christian Fellowship Publishers, 1986), 1-2.

MINISTRY CONTACT INFORMATION:

Jonathan Welton

www.WeltonAcademy.com